Passion, Fashion & Heart

Discover the unique ways to feel fabulous in your skin!

By Christina Kilmister

Published by

Heart Space Publications
PO Box 1085
Daylesford
Victoria
3460
Australia
Tel +61 450260348
www.heartspacebooks.com
pat@heartspacebooks.com

Copyright © 2018 Christina Kilmister
www.christinakilmister.com

Runway images by New York Photographer Katherine Angelique

Graphic Design: Felix Zamoranos of Ripped Box Station,
www.rippedboxstation.com

All rights reserved under international copyright conventions. No part of this book may be reproduced, stored in a retrieval system, or transmitted in any form or by any means electronic, mechanical, photocopying, recorded or otherwise without written permission from Heartspace Publications or Christina Kilmister.

Whilst every care has been taken to check the accuracy of the information in this book, the publisher cannot be held responsible for any errors, omissions or originality.

The Author's suggestions, ideas, tips, techniques and information in this book are not to be interpreted as a promise or guarantee. Every individual is different, and we therefore cannot guarantee your success or the attaining any results from using the given information. Nor are we responsible for any of your actions. All statements and suggestions in this book are the author's opinion only, and are given in an advisory capacity. However, it is likely that by following the principles in this book that the reader will improve on fashion sense for her own circumstances.

Published in 2018 at Melbourne

ISBN 978-0-6484889-0-3

About the Author

C hristina is from a Greek background and the youngest of four sisters, growing up in New Zealand.

Her mother sewed garments from a young age, and her mother also had a great love for all things fashion. So it is no surprise Christina has emulated that same passion through the generations.

Christina obtained a diploma in Fashion Design and Fashion Styling then went on to start her own business.

With being a young mum of two at the time, she soon found that she couldn't devote the time needed to her rapidly growing business and decided to join the family business for more balance.

Passion, Fashion & Heart

After several years, Christina moved into a corporate role, but realized some years later she was missing her true passion:- Fashion. She walked away from a corporate career to follow her heart. Christina is now founder/fashion designer of her own brand Lilika Designs (named after her mother).

Christina knew this was her purpose, she was here to empower and inspire the sisterhood, through fashion. She wanted women to feel special, fabulous in their skin. Bringing out their inner "Queen", to love themselves, follow their heart and live the ultimate life they love.

That is why she was driven to tell her own personal story, with the ups and downs, all she discovered and learnt from her experiences. What it takes to chase your dream and do what you love. She wears her heart on her sleeve and shares it all.

A whirlwind and amazingly special journey unfolded resulting in invtations to showcase all over the world including Paris, London, Milan and New York. Features in renowned fashion magazines- ELLE, Harpers Bazaar, Cosmopolitan and more.

When Christina is not designing, styling and running her brand, she is with her other true loves. Husband Bevan, children Timothy, Lily-Rose and her long time horse- Atlas.

Contact Christina- christina@christinakilmister.com
www.christinakilmister.com

Dedication and Thanks

This book was written with passion, love, honesty, an abundant happiness, and gratitude for my life. I chose this career, lost it, then found it again because I was driven to want to help other women – simply so they can feel better about themselves, the wonderful human beings that they are, love and cherish themselves inside and out.

That was, is and always will be my only reason for doing what I do.

Only you can decide what you want to do with your life.

Ultimately, of course, it is your decision. In saying that, the people surrounding you choose to either support and encourage you, or not. Those special ones who know you, they can see the fire burning in you, the relentless drive and resilience that pushes you forward, to make change happen.

Others call you a dreamer, and make you feel as if you are chasing some "fantasy", an unobtainable thing, that isn't quite real enough to do. They think that maybe you should be just doing a "normal" job. One that you may hate, but hey it's work and you're not meant to love your work, right? Yet we spend the majority of our lives at this "work". Most times, it is more then we spend at home with our loved ones. So why shouldn't we be doing something that we love? Who says it should be that way? Nobody says, only YOU.

Look at those people who try to put you off and plant doubt and question – are they people that inspire you? Do they make you want to live life to the fullest? Are they getting up every day and living their passion, doing what they love? More importantly, what are they actually doing in THEIR life to be able to question yours? I am amazingly blessed to have people around me that, firstly, want to be there for me, and secondly love me unconditionally.

If I hadn't been brought up being told it's ok to chase your dreams, to follow your heart, to try things until you find what you love – to be told there is no such thing as failure, which just meant that I hadn't yet found what it is I was meant to do with my life. All my so called failures led me to my dream job and life. If not, I wouldn't be writing this.

My parents gave me the love, encouragement and support, and most importantly the freedom to choose my own path. When I told them what I wanted to do, many called it my "latest obsession" or rolled their eyes and said, 'Here we go again, what's she doing this time?' There was nothing but love and excitement from my parents to see where it led. My mother Lily has the gentlest kindest soul and is the best mother in the world. She told me one day that after she lost her mother, she vowed to herself that one day she would be the best mother in the world. She definitely has that title, hands down. She has been beside me every step of the way.

My Dad (Richard), has always been my biggest supporter and fan, even to this day. Nothing is ever too much for my parents. They are both my best friends.

My children Timothy and Lily-Rose, keep me inspired to prove to them that in life you can do whatever you want. It's not about words, it's actions that counts. They have never heard the words, 'You can't do that' from me. I believe that is the biggest crusher of a person's soul. What I love may not be what someone else loves because we are totally different human beings.

The love for my children is something that drives me to be the best I can be. To be the best role model I can be. For them to believe in themselves, to live a life every day that they love. That is what I want for them. They are the best things I've ever had. I could not be more proud of the strong, kind and amazing adults they have become.

My husband Bevan who came into my life and stole my heart when I least expected it, and when I never thought I would love again. Showing me that one can find their perfect mate, the true love they were meant to grow old with. He stepped into the role of being "Dad" to my kids in one of the hardest times of their lives, was kind and supportive, whilst giving them the unconditional love that he has for them. He fell for them after he fell for me, not something at the time they would have believed. Without children before he met me, this was a role he blindly stepped into trying to find his own way, while the kids were also trying to find theirs. He allows me to be myself, which I have learnt over the years, must be the biggest gift you can give to someone you love. Not trying to change an ounce of them. Giving them the right to be their own person. He has encouraged and supported me to follow my heart, he has "carried" us so I can carry Lilika through to its success. He had the faith that I could build this business from the ground up. He is my buddy in life.

My dear friend Sheryl of over twenty years has watched me grow from a young mother through many stages of my life. Trying, "failing" and succeeding through different ventures. Always my greatest fan in whatever I chose to do. That's why she was there on my first journey with Lilika. She was meant to be.

My grandmother Christina, whom I sadly never had the opportunity to meet, is one of my biggest inspirations in my designing. How I would have loved to have known her. How proud she would have been of the person her beloved daughter grew up to be. The picture of her in my mind's eye is never far away during those times. I have her name. I am designing as she used to. She is there watching over me and my mother when we work together. Lilika is a part of her, as is my mother.

All these loved ones in my life are the ones I dedicate this book to. They are the people who have never let me down, had faith in me all the way. They have only ever backed me, given me the wings to fly and the freedom to follow my heart. Thank you… and I love you more than you will ever know.

My inspirational and amazing mentor- Peggy McColl

My wonderful readers- this is for you, whoever you are, wherever you are around the globe. From my heart to yours, it is because of you that I was inspired to write this book. I wanted to share my journey with the sisterhood, to help you in any way I can. So you can feel beautiful inside and out.

Christina xx

Testimonials

Christina is a rising-star designer and author of this delightful book packed with honest advice, inspirational ideas and self-examining lessons. You'll just love her funny, raw and honest voice.

Christina shares about her personal life, visions and dreams. She shares about the hard knocks, and just how she dusted herself off to keep on going for what she know was her designing destiny. It's her unpretentious ideas about body type and colour palette that empower the modern-woman to look her best whether casual or fancy anywhere anytime. Because when you finally get it right about what looks best on you, there's no stopping a confident woman, now is there ...

Tami Smith
Communication Skills Coach & Special Event Presenter
Los Angeles, California

One of the most informative styling books I have come across to date. Need some styling advice on topics such as body shapes, colour palettes and skin tones? This book covers all the basics along with a true reflection of Christina's pure determination to succeed within the fashion world. An inspiring and uplifting read which will excite any true fashionista as well give a few little giggles along the way. You want to know how to look and feel amazing? Then you definitely need this book in your life!

Saffron Edwards
First Class Qualified Stylist
United Kingdom

This book is amazing and I love it! I think many woman of all ages will find this an inspiring, empowering and fun read. Her journey is about listening to your heart, showing you that dreams do come true. With real life stories and great easy tips on styling. A must read that is hard to put down!

Monica Villar
Founder of Amanda Chic
Influencer, fashion, travel and lifestyle blogger
Spain

As an internationally renowned celebrity fashion designer in Beverly Hills, I speak from the heart when I say "This is one woman that needs to be watched! Her dedication, persistence and absolute love for what she does, makes you want to read chapter after chapter without putting it down."

By the time you have finished this book, you will want to call her up, have a chat and go out for a shop or drink! That is how she makes you feel, like you are already best friends. She is real, she hides nothing and she gives her all. Her zany and confident personality grabs you the moment you start to read. Her love for wanting to help other women feel good, wanting everyone to know that you can have everything that you ever wanted in life, gives you a totally satisfying and feel good read, that leaves you wanting more.

Packed fabulously full of great advice that comes from the heart. Yes she writes about her designs on the catwalks of the world fashion industry and backstage antics but this book is not really about those glamorous times – they are about you, the shop assistant, the student, business woman, and of course the stay-at-home mum. This is one for your coffee table, for your friends and family. You will take something away from this book. When you have finished the book, you will want to pick it up and read it again and continue to learn and grow from her experiences

Pol' Atteu
Celebrity Fashion Designer
TV Personality, Gown and Out in Beverly Hills
Beverly Hills, California

Collection Showcase

Dressing myself every day was a chore, with trying on several outfits or combinations… all having the same result; where I looked just "drab". It got the point where I wouldn't even fight it anymore, I knew that whatever I chose from my closet was just going to make me look "ordinary", but Christina's book changed all that. I'm fifty and now feel like I'm in my 20s! The clothes I choose make me look and feel fabulous! I was doing exactly what some of the women were doing in Christina's book, NOT dressing for my body shape and accentuating my less desirable features. Choosing clothes and dressing my body shape based on Christina's advice has given me a "WOW" factor.

I have never received so many compliments on the way I look in such a short period of time. It's truly left me in a state of "I don't know how to reply" when people compliment me..eg., saying "that cold shoulder sweater" looks so nice on you, you look so nice in those in jeans; "wearing my big pocket jeans" People are actually thinking that I have got work done. My friend Anna said she overheard one of the soccer mom's say "I think she got a breast enlargement" and "I have to find out what her diet is". My diet was Christina's book. If you are not getting compliments on the way you look….Christina's book is food for thought!

Maria Sullivan
New Hampshire, United States
CEO of International Business Connect
Industry Innovator Award by IT Event Magazine
Named Top 20 influencer of Women in IT by Inc. Magazine

This book is wonderful and exceptional in every way. Christina's insightful comments and great tips on Fashion and styling are so helpful, inspiring and entertaining, I could not put it down! She has gone for what she truly wants to do in her life without limiting herself to what people might think is "possible". I think this book empowers many of us to create the life you choose to live and feel good about it.

Yura Lyvv alias Sarah Anna
Fashion Designer
Influencer
TV Host

The energy of this book and Christina's personality was wonderful - she's such an Inspirational woman but most of all, and best of all she's very real. This book is obviously written from the heart. Her message is so inspiring and for me, trying to follow my passion of becoming a full-time editor, her emphasis on hope, determination and perseverance is spot on. The section on style is very clear, useful and full of handy tips! I really enjoyed this one.

All the best,

Maddy Mcglynn
Editor
Canada

This book is a fabulous read that I think many people can relate to. Christina's Journey of making the real life, brave decision, to walk away from a corporate career, to chase her long lost "love" In the fashion industry shows her character and resilience. Like her designs, that are truly unique, she has the same approach to life of not letting anything hold her back. With her fun, honest, Infectious personality, I admire all she has achieved on her path to success, and In such a short time.

We can all take something away from this book, whether it be styling, finding your own way, your true love, or simply just having the hope that you too can be doing what you want In life. Be empowered and Inspired as this is one book you won't want to put down. I'm hoping there is a second one in the making very soon!

Coco Chanel said; "In order to be Irreplaceable one must always be different". And Christina Is different.

Jing Song
Multi Award Winning Founder &
Managing Director of Crown Range Cellar
New Zealand

Welcome to Christina and her journey, as she refreshingly opens up her world to you on a platter. How she followed her heart, wouldn't give up and how it led to living her dream. This book is a fun and fresh, it oozes real life ups and downs, and written with a true and raw passion that is rarely seen these days. Christina mimics my persona in life by not being afraid to show her true love in life. No matter what. Showing you how to look and feel fabulous whatever shape you have.

She is an inspiration and empowers as she delivers laugh, tears, and those "OMG"! Moments that will pull at your heart strings. This is not just about fashion, it is about self-esteem and acceptance, and learning to love yourself.

Patrik Simpson
TV Personality, Gown and Out in Beverly Hills
Beverly Hills, California

Move over Carrie Bradshaw...Aotearoa has their own fashionista diva in Christina Kilmister. Her first book, *"Passion, Fashion and Heart"* is the definitive how to guide for fashion, following your heart and being happy in your own skin. Christina's writing style grabs you from the first paragraph, it is raw, honest and emotional – but most of all it is entertaining. I love the amusing anecdotes of her life, which lead to important fashion lessons and tips we can all take on board. And the Fab Five's stories pull at heart strings as we can all relate to experiences where we felt totally out of place in our own bodies. Read on to find out how Christina teaches Emma, Mandy, Jayne, Alice and Georgie to take charge of their appearance and make the most out of their body shapes. On her way to taking the global fashion scene by storm with Lilika Designs, this is one woman who knows what she wants and how to get it. This book is a must read for all of us looking to find our inner posh and become the woman we all know we are inside!

Leigh O'Connor
Writer - AGFG
Queensland, Australia

Contents

About the Author iii

Dedication and Thanks v

Testimonials viii

It's All About Amazing YOU! xiv

Part One

The Fabulous Five 2

Lilika – My posh little monster 15

I'm No Cookie Cutter 52

Moments 90

Part two

When to say YES – When to say NO – When to say Never Ever! 97

Could have – Should have – Would have 114

My Fashion Emergency LBB 132

Perfect Color – Make it Pop, Shine and Glow 144

What Lies Beneath… 154

Fact File – Shape n Style 161

A Sprinkle of this and A Dash of that 173

It's All About Fabulous YOU! 184

Christina Kilmister

You finally find the time to duck into a clothing store, most probably squeezed into your limited lunch hour or that small window before or after school pickup, to scan for anything that may pop out at you…Yes! You see something… pulling it off the rack, you race into the dressing room and try it on… possibly… maybe, you have found something that you like… Short-lived – it doesn't fit right, it doesn't look right, you know it doesn't, even if the sales girl is telling you it looks great!

It's true, isn't it? How many times have we gone into a store and played out that scenario, at some stage of our lives? Some more than others.

Yes, we want beautiful clothes. Yes, we want them to fit like a glove, and yes we all want to wear something that highlights those glorious womanly parts of our body, and make us feel fabulous…to dazzle wherever we go. Is that seriously too much to ask? But how do we do it?

At twenty-two, I was a young mother of two, with a son and daughter, so I am aware of the lifestyle this entails. As a mum, you still want to feel and look great, especially now, as you race around, balancing a thousand things, wearing multiple hats, all in one day. Why should you still not feel and look great? Our jobs, whether we are mothers at home or working, maybe both, or a professional trying to juggle your boss's workload, running your own business, whatever it may be, we are not always left that much ME time. If I could I do it all over again, I would have made sure I focused more on this.

If you are 100% committed with yourself, you will only be that and more to your family and loved ones. And I'm sure they would prefer that rather then you running around, feeling un-fabulous and deprived of all things womanly, while you are looking after your family, or your boss for that matter. Hmmm, food for thought...right? Make it a strawberry cupcake topped with cream cheese icing.

I have digressed a little, but even so, you may have already picked up that this is something I am passionate about, and believe it is important as a woman to look after you, no matter what your role in life may be. So when you are standing in that store, and you did actually find something that you liked, but it just didn't look how you thought it would on your body, when you are staring at this reflection in the mirror maybe even wishing that it wasn't yours, you just hung it back up and walked out, thinking I will shop another time.

NO! Back up that bus! Read on and let me help you decipher and try to make sense on how we should dress, how we can get to know our body a little bit better, so we can start saying 'yes, you gorgoeus woman, that's perfect, I'll buy it in every color!'

This book is about YOU, but first let me share with you how my story started, or should I say how my obsession with fashion began. I am one of four sisters, and the baby. I grew up with my mother sewing the most beautiful clothes for my sisters and I. Many nights I would go to sleep hearing her machine purring, then her sneaking quietly in to my room to lay an item on the end of my bed – her latest creation for either myself or my dolls.

Pretending to be fast asleep, I would fight the urge to take a sneak peek after the door had closed. I silently told myself I truly had the best mother in the world. So that would be my surprise in the morning, the moment I opened my eyes I would throw my blankets off and scoot down the end of the bed to see my new additions.

Mother loved all things fashion, just like her own mother, who also designed and sewed gorgeous creations. Always dressing my Mother so beautifully, this was so clear to see in the old photos.

Sadly she died when my mother was only seven, so she did not get to experience that wonderful relationship with her mother, like I now have with mine. She still talks often of my Grandmother. The few memories she has of her, she treasures and shares with me. Many of them are connected to fashion in one way or another. It is a very special bond we have together.

I spent a lot of time with my mother, as my older sisters were at school. She adored shopping the fabric shops (looking back, it was possibly a slight addiction), and I was her little shadow. I would play – sitting immersed in fabrics, trims and buttons dressing my dolls.

So naturally as soon as my foot could touch the pedal I was bought my very own, super shiny new sewing machine, and then I was the one sewing clothes for my mother! The machine was a beautiful, rich cream, just like a block of butter. I was so proud of it and would polish it with a little square of fabric I had made and dedicated to it. This had a bright pink

My grandmother Christina and my mother Lily.

My mother (aged four here) with just one of her many frocks Grandmother would make her.

zigzag stitch around the outside (even then loving my pinks). How the tables had been turned. The pure delight on her face when I would turn up with a new outfit for her! It melted my heart, for all she had done for me. It seemed so little but clearly meant so much to her. I also now have my mother's sewing machine that I sew all my first sketch samples on, yes I could get a more modern machine. No way. I had watched my mother for hours sewing on this machine growing up and now it was part of me and my brand. I remember when I was little, longing to be big enough one day to have her machine.

To this day she is always included in my collections. We have such fun together and she is my biggest fan. She was the one, who on my very first collection, hand sewed all the beautiful buttons on every single sample design that had them on. I must now confess, I adore buttons, could say maybe obsessed. Mum always had a huge jar full of all shapes, sizes, and colors. To me, it was like a glorious candy jar packed with delectable treats. Even now, I always design with buttons for that finishing detail – these have become my brand's trademark.

Anyway, back to my story; many years later when I had my own children, I discovered I was still in love with fashion, to be fair, madly in love, designing and putting together outfits for myself and my daughter in any spare time I had. Most times it was late at night while the kids were asleep. One night, even dozing off at my machine and dropping my foot onto the pedal, waking up in a complete panic with the machine speeding along, and heading straight for my fingers!

Another deviation; a friend of mine had just recently got into modelling and was about to start a modelling /etiquette course. She talked me into going along with her, thought it would be fun for us to both do it together. To get any closer, or be a part of anything that entailed fashion, got me very excited. It was evening classes so it worked out well with the kids. After the course I ended up getting some modelling work through an agency on a part time basis. It was a contact that had come through the course. It was the next best thing for me as I got to dress up in style and have some fun. I had been booked one weekend to be part of a fashion show. That day arrived and when I got there I went backstage. There were heaps of chairs and hair/makeup teams already there waiting for us. We were told to just pick a chair and they would get started. I keep walking along, not really knowing why (I could have just picked the first empty chair I had seen in front of me). Then I stopped and saw a gorgeous dark haired lady, beautiful makeup and some super stylie pants with a top that definitely had the amount of bling on it that I love. She turned fully around at that moment, and looked straight at me with a huge welcoming smile. Yip… the perfect chair. I sat down, and with a voice full of bubbled excitement, and she burst out, 'hello girl'.

From that moment we didn't stop talking, but she said at one point, 'Wow, it just feels like I have known you for years. After this show let's meet up and do a photo shoot together. I will dolly you all up, and we will get some new portfolio shots for you'.

I said, 'Yes I would love that!' So we exchanged numbers and started making plans for where we would shoot and what clothes I would bring to wear. She turned out to be a great photographer, as well as a hair and makeup artist. We shared more about each other, stories and giggled almost the whole way through the rest of our time together. When she had finished my fabulous hair and makeup, I gave her a big hug before I went on stage.

She said, 'I am so happy that you chose my chair'. I walked away and thought to myself, well everything happens for a reason that's for sure. Her name is Sheryl, and I did not know when I sat down in front of her that day what a great impact she would have on my life. That she would get to know my kids, would do my hair and makeup for many years to come, see me get married, be like a loving big sister and become one of my dearest friends. She loved style, bling, fashion and dressing up as much as me (well close). We were kindred spirits and both felt it. Twenty years later we are still laughing and have been on so many adventures together I have lost count. The photo shoots we have done together are out of the ball park. She is all about living life to the fullest and has the same mentality as me with getting out there and just doing what she wants to do. You will hear more about this lovely fun lady later on.

Anyway, again, back again to the story… I had always wanted to make an effort and look good, not just for myself but for my family, I wanted to pick my kids up from school and have them be proud of me, not having to hide around the corner until everyone else had gone, before taking my hand and walking to the car. I must say however, that was at least until we came closer to the teenage years.

I would make sure I always did that school drop off and pick up looking nice and they were my favorite times of day where I got to wear the new clothes I had designed and made. YET I got many looks up and down, disapproving glares, and whispers and snickers from other mothers.

Let me make this clear, when I said I made an effort, I mean I wore something pretty, appropriate of course, and always had my hair brushed. I think they thought I should have just been wearing something super casual. I mean, why should we bother to look good just to pick our kids up right? I wanted to show my kids that it is important to look after yourself and be proud of who you are.

One day I was getting my daughter's bag from the cloakroom and I had a mother come up to me. She was in bright trackies and an oversized white shirt and runners. Bless her soul she looked exhausted and a little sad.

She said to me with a gentle smile, 'I just wanted to tell you that you always look so lovely each day. I know the other mothers treat you unkindly, and I really don't know why they are like that. So I just wanted to tell you that'.

My heart went out to her, she had taken the time to come over and tell me those kind words.

She then asked, 'How do you do it? Like you, I have two kids but I just can't get myself together. I have no motivation, I just don't know what to do with myself or where to start. I know I have only just properly met you, but I feel like I can ask you. Will you please help me?'

Then and there I realized, this is something I want to do and maybe something I need to change. Then it hit me, are those other mothers just feeling the same? Do we all just need to help each other? It made me think that just a simple thing like making sure you had the time to look after yourself was actually quite crucial.

I said to Emma (I will never forget her even after all these years), 'How about we have a play date?' She looked a little surprised I had actually agreed. Meanwhile, I couldn't believe how excited I was at the prospect of going to Emma's. I felt like a child that had just been told she had free rein of Willy Wonkers!

Several days later after getting her measurements, and some late night sewing with lots of coffee, I took the kids around to her place for our play date. She had the cutest white cottage with a white picket fence. She had a great big closet that to my utter delight, was crammed full of clothes. Oh the joy, I was in a happy place that I hadn't known existed. What an awesome time we had. The kids got on well and became instant friends. Let's just say I pretty much invaded and reinvented her closet, and made her over, then dressed her up in the clothes I had created especially for her and had an absolute ball doing it. Even then I didn't quite realize my love for styling, but more importantly, it was about HELPING someone feel good about themselves.

That was the key, that's what drove me. The look on her face when she saw her hair and makeup and slipped on her brand new outfits… it was the best thing ever. She burst into tears.

'You will never know what you have done for me. I feel so good, and from now on I'm going to look after myself'. She ran out to find her daughters and show them her new clothes and look. The girls squealed with happiness for their mummy and told her how pretty she looked.

I was a little puzzled, after all, all we had done was to have some girly time. I had played with her hair and makeup, dressed her up, and had great fun going through her closet. How can that be so life changing?

She told me she didn't know where to start or what to do, she thought people would laugh at her if she tried to make herself look a little better. Yet here was a beautiful woman, with a beautiful soul to match, who just needed a little direction and support, someone to tell her it was ok to do something for her. Feeling good is the beginning of feeling amazing in other areas of your life. That I have learnt.

The following week Emma and her hubby went out on a date night, for the first time in three years. He actually rung me up a few days later and said, 'I just wanted to thank you, my lovely confident and happy wife is back'. I really couldn't believe that something SO small could be so important. I decided then and there that this was something I needed to take further, so I decided to study it. I obtained a diploma in fashion design. But that wasn't enough. I went on to complete a diploma in fashion styling. Then of course me being me, I wanted to have my own business, so I set up my very first brand, a boutique based at home.

Long story short, it was a huge success and got to the point it was so busy that I struggled with time for my family. My son and daughter were still young at the time. But I had to "make the call". At that stage, family came first and it still does, so I put the business on hold and moved into the family business in property. Several years later I got offered a corporate role within the same industry. More years later I realized I was no longer enjoying my job, I was successfully building someone else's business – I was miserable. But worse, it was taking its toll on my health. The only part of my day that I enjoyed was the mornings when I would decide what to wear to work. The girls at work were always commenting on my clothes and how I styled things together.

One day I collapsed at work from sheer exhaustion and stress. When the ambulance turned up, the medics were not happy with the results on their machine monitor. It showed an erratic heart. They wanted to admit me into hospital to monitor me for a while. I didn't want to go anywhere but they told me firmly they were not leaving me in this condition. My boss called my husband Bevan and told him what had happened. He came straight in, he was actually not working far away, which was unusual. He is a builder and normally worked on the other side of the city. He reached us just as they were about to carry me out on the stretcher. It was humiliating being carried through the building down the lifts, out through the café that was at the bottom floor of our building and onto the busy streets. I was thinking to myself, I mean, is all this really necessary?! They secured me inside and Bevan sat next to me. Apparently, my heart was skipping beats the whole way into the hospital. The medic guy said to me, 'You shouldn't be having this at your age'.

Oh charming, I thought. Thanks for that. Great to hear.

I was monitored for some time, and only after the doctors were satisfied would they release me. They gave me strict instructions of bedrest and told me to book in to see them again in a few days' time. They wanted me to get checked out regularly to keep an eye on things.

In the meantime, from the moment I was out of hospital I was asked when I would be back at work. Of course sales needed to be made, I felt instant pressure, a heaviness in my heart, guilt for actually being unwell, even though it was out of my control. My body had shut down. I had totally lost my mojo, mind, body and soul. I felt like I couldn't even allow myself the time to fully recover. I had a huge sense of responsibility to my work and company, where I have always been a hard worker, whatever it is I am doing I give it my all. I had given this job my all and clearly my body was telling me I had given too much! I knew myself there was no way my body was ready to jump back on the wheel again. My boss kindly gave me the time off, which was a huge load off my mind. It was taken out of my hands anyway, as the doctors ordered strict bed rest and that I was in no state to start back at work.

On following visits after the collapse, the doctor said to me one day, 'you need to get out of this job, the stress will kill you'. Wow… well that was profound, especially for a doctor. Was she seeing something I wasn't? Had I become that accustomed to running myself to the ground, that it had become normal? It had really made me take notice and question what I was doing and where I was going. Also what I wanted from life. I must admit, I had felt at times that I was just on a rat's wheel, going round and round and round.

I went home and that night had a big talk with Bevan. He is so level-headed, where as I tend to be more impulsive. So when he confessed how worried he had been about me and my health, I was surprised he was all for a life changing move. So I made the decision and that was it, I needed to make a change for myself and for my family. My "kids", although young adults at this stage, said to me, 'Do it Mum, it's your time now'.

Let me just say right now, I have been blessed with an amazing mother and father, husband and two kids, who are my inspiration. It is for them I put words into action to show them you can follow your heart, you can do what you love, and whatever you want to do in this life you can do it.

After some much needed rest and recovery, I thought, oh dear, what on earth do I do now? I asked myself three very important questions: What do I love? What am I good at? What would excite me to get out of bed in the morning and work (I am not a morning person). So it had to be pretty good. One single but beautiful and fabulous word…fashion! Instantly, I exploded with ideas, with possibilities. I filled up my notepad in a matter of minutes, with a happiness that I hadn't felt in a long time – I WAS BACK!

With that in mind, I knew I must create clothes that were chic, full of color and personality. The first words I got when I told my old colleagues what I was doing was where they scoffed, 'Good luck with that… the fashion industry is impossible to break into'. That just stoked the fire, as that comment empowered me in a way that was hard to describe. I had never felt so driven and so focused to succeed. It was often quite amusing how people would just assume it was a "one minute wonder". That this lady with the mop of long blonde hair who was obsessed with clothes and dressing up could possibly be serious enough and know enough to run her own business. I have always loved having blonde hair, it really is quite fun. It seems like one can get away with so much with the words, 'Oh, that was a blonde moment'.

Looking into the future for a moment – I had the opportunity to reply to one of these old colleagues as they ever so politely asked me, 'So how is your business? I knew full well that they had been following my brand and knew exactly what had been happening. Funny how things come back to you, isn't it? When I replied to them, with all the wonderful things that had happened, there was silence. Yip no response.

It was one of the biggest decisions, and also the scariest I have made but I did it. I walked away from what I call a "black and white" world, into one of color, one that I had been craving for a long time but really had no idea just how badly.

So here I am, many years later. I have come a full circle and found my way back to my passion, my true love that has always had my heart. So my label Lilika Designs was born, named after my beautiful mother who is also my best friend. Lilika is her name in Greek, and also my daughter's, whom I named after my mother. So it was perfect. My grandmother was also Christina, and I was given that special treasure of her name. Oh, and YES, I am part Greek, and you may notice this threaded throughout the book.

My inspiration comes from following my heart, and simply doing what I love, what makes me happy, and what makes a woman feel fabulous, going right back to when I dressed Emma for the very first time. I say to people, I don't get up in the morning and work, I get up and play.

With that in mind, I knew I must create clothes that were exclusive, luxurious to wear, chic, full of color and personality and with a touch of playfulness about them. I want women who wear my designs to feel special, to be the center of attention, to be unforgettable.

When a woman steps out onto the street in Lilika, she is not going to be wearing the same as everyone else. I never wanted anything more than a boutique label, never wanting to be a chain store, and that is something I have always been certain about.

You can have the most gorgeous clothes in the world, but knowing what to wear, and how to wear them, that's what makes clothes come to life on your body. There is more to just putting on a pretty dress, it is the way it makes you feel, makes you move, it is the power it gives you as a woman, mind, body, and soul. If you feel awesome – you are awesome. So making pieces that a busy woman could put together easily and effortlessly is important to me, so she could be her own stylist at home if need be. I wanted to design clothes that could be mixed and matched so when she stepped out to meet the world, whether it be the school drop off, or into the boardroom, she would look and feel fabulous.

Being comfortable, delivering gorgeous quality, luxurious and versatile designs was my hot button. There is nothing worse than looking fabulous but not feeling fabulous because it just isn't loving your body. I want you to stay in your dress from sunrise to sunset. So the fabrics I choose must pass my comfort test.

Christina Kilmister

Then I got to thinking, I need to write all this down. I knew years ago I would have loved to have been given a book stuffed full of delicious and fun tips, offering secrets on all things fashion that a girl loves and needs, about real women that I could relate to. I know Emma would have. Each time I would go over to her house, she would get her notebook out and write down what I was saying so she wouldn't forget it after I had gone.

I thought, if I am going to write this book it needs to be fun, easy to read, and be written with the true passion that I have for what I do – to just be me, I want it to feel like I am actually talking to you, with you, while we are having double mocha latte or a glass of wine sitting on a big comfy couch.

YES, I want it to be all about YOU, as a gorgeous woman, whether you are a mother, sister, girlfriend, partner, fiancé, wife or daughter…YOU, whoever you are, and whatever you do in life, this is about the sisterhood!

So buckle up and let's get started!

The Fabulous Five

Let me introduce my five lovely ladies, all with a personal story of the realization that they were not happy with how they felt or looked. I wanted to show by sharing these gorgeous women with you, from all walks of life, ages, experiences and body types. Sometimes we just need a little sprinkle of love, help and guidance.

Read on as they unveil their moments that made them say, 'No more… I want to do something. This is all about me!'

Firstly we have Emma… well, you already know a little about her as she was my first styling make over, and my inspiration to be doing what I am now.

Emma is in her mid-thirties, with dark brown hair that is super straight and well below the shoulders, large brown eyes framed by thick lashes that look fake, but aren't. She is married with two gorgeous girls, Sally and Ella, five and seven years old. She works as a part time administrator in a doctor's surgery. Her husband John is a computer technician and works for a large corporation in the city. They have been together for twelve years and live in a quiet suburb on the shores of Auckland.

Emma has the body shape that is best known as The Pear, which is all about balance! Balance between your top, and your bottom. With this shape, it is best to keep the focus on your lovely slim top, and the rest will naturally follow.

The key to remember for the pear are the thighs. My, don't we all love that word! The pear shape may seem like she has wide hips, but actually, it's the thighs where the width is.

To create a body that appears more balanced, you will need to take emphasis away from the thigh area, and draw it up to the top part of the body – that nice slimmer part.

A little later we can go into more detail on the shapes, but for now let's look at Emma's moment of pain, the one that pushed her to make a change about how she felt about herself. This was prior to meeting me. After hearing her story, you will understand why at the school that day she asked for my help. I am so happy that I gave it.

Emma had just arrived at the school to pick up the girls, where she found her oldest daughter Ella in tears. Sally was with her and patting her gently on the arm a little awkwardly, not quite knowing what to do but clearly worried about her big sister. Emma ran up to her. 'What happened? Are you hurt?'

Ella, upon seeing her mum, quickly wiped her tears away, and with a very good effort on her part summoned a smile.

'I'm fine Mummy'. Clearly, something upset her, dreadfully. But out of the corner of her eye, she saw several girls, in a tightly-knit group walking away, chattering and giggling, whilst looking back over their shoulders.

She asked Ella, 'Did those girls upset you?'

Ella replied, 'Mummy it's ok… let's go home, I'm really hungry!'

Emma then looked over at Sally who was shifting a little uncomfortably from foot to foot but decided to leave it until they got home before she would gently delve into this.

After they arrived back, an afternoon snack was prepared, and Ella was settled doing homework in her room. Emma took her opportunity to ask Sally, 'What upset Ella today, darling? Did those girls that walked away when I turned up have anything to do with this?'

Sally, with head down, hesitated, but then looked up and nodded her head. 'What did they say?' Emma asked. Sally, barely audible said, 'Mean things about you, Mummy'.

'What on earth… oh! ... my goodness'. Emma didn't know what she had been expecting, but certainly not this.

Sally's bottom lip started to quiver until she broke down crying… her little shoulders shaking. The poor child didn't want to say another word.

Emma's smart and decided to leave the matter for then. She wasn't pushing her, not until one of them felt they could talk about it. But then all of a sudden, Sally blurted out, 'They were telling Ella that you were fat and had big legs, like an elephant, and that you couldn't fit your pants properly!'

Emma felt like she'd been kicked in the gut and died a little inside. Well not just a little, a lot. What does one say to that? She was mortified, ashamed, and angry. This was not only for herself, but the fact that her daughters had to deal with this, and hear such things about their mother. She knew children can be cruel and harsh, but this was devastating.

She gave Sally a tight hug, and a kiss on the forehead. And as she wiped her tears, she said, 'We don't listen to mean girls… do we darling?' Sally shook her little head, her blonde curls bouncing from side to side, as Emma, with wisdom born from sadness said, 'If you don't have anything nice to say…'

'…Don't say anything.' 'Exactly,' Emma agreed.

For the first time, Sally smiled and asked, 'Can I have some more cookies Mummy?' Clearly, that moment had passed. Phew.

With that over, Sally nestled into the beanbag, almost swallowing her little frame, as she watched her favorite programme. Emma slipped quietly into her room and stood in front of the mirror.

'What happened to you?' she questions the reflection in the mirror. 'Those kids are right', she says out loud. 'I do look like an elephant in these pants… and now I feel like one too.'

She looked at herself brutally and honestly for the first time in a very long time, with her tight leggings that were a soft baby pink, which she loved. She considered the big flower pockets at the front, just down from the hips. Next, she looked up at her baggy shapeless, same color, sweatshirt – it was just so comfortable, and the length was perfect for her, almost covering her bottom. She let out a long sigh.

She had THOUGHT she dressed OK. But thinking about it she knew she couldn't be bothered and went for comfort. After all, life was all about the kids, and John. Come to think of it, she and John don't really do much together as a couple and hadn't for ages, too much to juggle with work, the girls, and the house to take care of. That was sad. She wondered if John thought that she looked like an elephant too? Oh, she couldn't bear to tell him what happened today, it was degrading enough hearing it once, and she just couldn't repeat it. She was sure the girls weren't going to bring it up again anytime soon either. It was upsetting enough for Sally having to tell her.

Emma said out loud to the mirror, 'I need to do something, this today with those girls has made me realize that underneath, I'm not happy with how I look or feel, it has forced me to be truthful with myself. I have pushed my feelings aside for too long… but where do I start? Oh forget it, it is just too overwhelming. I don't even know what to do anyway. I'm sure people would just laugh at any attempts I made.'

She headed back out to the kitchen to start preparations for dinner.

NOW, what do you think Emma should be wearing? You will have to wait and see...

Next meet Mandy

She is in her early thirties with sandy shoulder length, wavy hair, a pale complexion, lovely blue eyes, and a pert little nose, topped with a sprinkle of freckles.

She lives with her partner Simon and their three boys, two year old Jacob, four year old Carl and seven year old Davie. She is a full time mum and Simon is a mechanic with his own business. They live just out of town on a small lifestyle block in the country.

Mandy has the body shape known as – The Apple.

The apple (if you are one) is best described as round, in other words, your waist is not defined, and is your widest part. But you have a great bust, so make the most of it and focus upstairs not downstairs! That is your tactic; you need to get your tummy in proportion and lessen the impact on the rest of your frame. A clear definition is what you need between your boobs and your tummy.

I will tell you more about this shape a little later, but for now, I will share with you Mandy's embarrassing moment that drove her to know it was time to make a change.

Mandy is fed up of being uncomfortable, looking drab and feeling like a hippo (her words), and it got to the point where it was a stress for her to get dressed in the mornings and think of what to wear. Ever since her most painful moment last year, she has lost even more motivation than before, and had almost given up trying. This is what happened…

Mandy and Simon had organized a dinner for the end of year with their employees from the garage and their families. They put on something each year at this time before the big Christmas holidays.

Mandy decided she would make an effort and wear a nice dress. She felt herself getting excited for the first time in a little while. She was sure she had read in a magazine somewhere that wearing a good tight dress helped suction all those wayward rolls. It made sense, she thought.

She knew she had a dress just like that too, somewhere, hidden away in that big dark hole called her closet. It had got to be somewhere in there, and it would fit the bill perfectly.

She hated shopping as she never had any idea what to look for, and when she did try something on it never looked how she thought it would. So she would either walk out empty handed or on some random impulse buy, and it just went into the closet, until one day, like today.

After rummaging around she found it, yes! There it was, ha-ha, and as anticipated, the tags were still on. Impulse buy for sure. It was white with a high neck and super tight, and sitting above the knee in length. It looked rather like a pipe. She wasn't sure if that was a good thing or a bad thing. Anyway, on it goes.

It was difficult for her to get it on, it was so tight and small but that was the idea, it expanded perfectly once she got it over her neck. She didn't remember the neck being so high though, but that surely would make her neck look lovely and elegant. What would life be without a good stretch fabric? Oh, Simon was going to be blown away with her look tonight.

She found some black stiletto heels. Should you wear black shoes with a white dress? Hmmm… oh well, that will do. She then found a lovely pink shoulder bag that would fit all her bits and pieces in exactly right. After adding her makeup and brushing her hair she was ready to go! Great timing, the babysitter Carly had just rung the door bell. Simon had also texted saying he was already at the restaurant, she was meeting him there.

Mandy was looking forward to some kid-free time with Simon.

After saying goodbye to Carly, and running through a few things with her, she left. About half an hour later, she had arrived at the venue and found the group of employees and their families. She hadn't met all the other wives yet, as a couple of new employees had come on during the year. She didn't get the time to pop into the garage much, not like she used to. Sometimes she would surprise Simon and just turn up with some freshly made muffins for their morning tea. He had always loved those visits.

She found Simon with a beer in hand and talking away, when he first looked over and saw her, he had looked so surprised, she thought he was going to drop his beer! His mouth hung open, which was just the reaction she wanted.

'Wow you look …um… different!' She walked up and gave him a peck on the cheek.

'Thanks honey,' she said happily.

Just then one of the wives came up, who looked like she was about eight months pregnant, introduced herself. She was accompanied by her eight or nine year old daughter. The daughter, whose name I was told was Kylie, first looked at Mandy, then turned to her mother and said in a loud voice, 'oh look Mum she is having a baby too, just like us!'

Her mother said, 'Yes, how wonderful… when is your due date?' And with a lovely smile on her face, continued, 'you look like you are not too far away'.

Suddenly, you could have heard a tissue drop. Emma looked at Simon, who in turn looked like he had just seen a ghost. As you can imagine, Mandy almost turned the color of her pink bag, whilst unconsciously grabbing at her stomach. Smiling awkwardly, and totally wanting in that very moment to be swallowed into the ground, topped with a truckload of soil, never to come out again, mumbled something incoherent about having to call the babysitter. She turned and fled as fast as she could but also as calmly as she could possibly muster. Once through the door where no one could see her, she broke into a run and headed for the car park. She could hear Simon calling out for her.

'Mandy, Mandy, darling please stop!'

By the time she reached the car door her face was drenched with tears. She jumped in the car, quickly turned on the engine and sped out of the park, glancing in the rear view mirror and seeing Simon standing there, raking his hands through his hair as the car disappeared.

Feeling at her lowest point, she had tried so hard to get it all right and make Simon proud of her, whilst having a great night out. Instead, she had been a huge humiliation to him… his big fat partner. No wonder he hadn't asked her to marry him after all these years. Why would he? Now on top of that, she had left him alone at the party.

She had never felt so embarrassed, in front of all their employees. Oh, she never wanted to look any of them in the face ever again. Poor Kylie, she had no idea the bomb she just dropped, the poor mother too, being the wife of a newbie, was probably at this point feeling pretty uncomfortable about the whole situation. She was sure by now one of the other women would have told her that Mandy was not pregnant.

"Why did I even bother?" she said out loud to herself. What the worst thing was was that she had actually thought she looked really good! How could she have got it so wrong? What does she do now apart from booking herself into a cosmetic surgeon and ordering him to suck everything out of her, which certainly was not going to happen anytime soon. She knew she had to do something. She glanced down again at her stomach in the super stretchy fabric, sitting on her lap like a sack of spuds. Ha, the thought back to her idea of the dress keeping the rolls in.

'Sucks it all in aye, yeah right!' She vowed in that moment she was never, ever going to be humiliated again about her body. She was going to do something about it, starting straight away.

NOW, what SHOULD Mandy have been wearing? Soon you will hear…

Say hello to Jayne

She is in her late twenties, has honey blonde hair that sits half way down her back, green eyes, and gorgeous high cheek bones. She works part-time as a PA in a legal firm while she is in her fifth year of a law degree. She lives in a city apartment, so it is nice and near to the university and her work. Currently, she is happily single and feels that she doesn't have the time to commit to a relationship, all her extra time and energy is spent on her studies. For now, this is just the way she likes it. The previous relationships were hard work, the men either couldn't cope with her workload or they were just too needy. It was working well now.

Jayne's body shape is the – Strawberry/Inverted Triangle/Lollipop.

The shape has a generous bust, wider shoulders, long legs, and slim waist and hips (yes-hello!), which are the defining features of this shape. The key is balancing the figure and de-emphasizing the upper half, so there is no top-heavy look.

Believe it or not, if you have this shape you need to subtly broaden the hips and accentuate the waist.

Before I tell you more about this shape though, let me share with you Jayne's realization of needing to know how to dress the right way to save any more mortifying moments.

It was her twenty-ninth birthday and she had just unwrapped a present from her best friend to discover a super tight bright pink top with a high neck with little bling all around it. It was her favorite style, her friend knew her so well, and it used to be her favorite style…oh no… it was all coming back to her…

About six months earlier, she was at work one day on her computer putting together a summary for her boss when ding! A new message popped into her mailbox.

She looked at the address box and it was from one of the guys in another department… Eric, on a different floor of their office building – why would he be emailing her?! He had only ever said hello in passing in the lift to their office floor, which was, come to think of it, nearly every morning. Him and his friend.

She opened the email and started reading….and reading and reading… her hands fell away from the keyboard and she sat back in her chair. One of the girls walking past her desk asked, 'Jayne? Are you OK? You look like you have just seen a ghost!' Jayne replied, without turning her head. 'Yes fine, Margo just thinking…'.

How could she ever face Eric and his work mate again? This was awful… he had obviously sent this email to her by mistake instead of his friend Sean, she started at the top of the email again and slowly, painfully re-read it.

'Another exciting day to see what our resident hottie Jayne is wearing today! That must be a new top, haven't seen that one before, the guys are all betting that she won't be able to walk upright by the end of the day with that big rack weighing her down, ha-ha, not that we mind! It's always a great part of the day when Jayne arrives. The only lady in town that really gives the boys something to look at. I hear too that she is studying to be a lawyer. I bet the court room will be packed out when she starts practicing, she will have new clients lining up at her office door. Ha-ha'.

Devastated, she just wanted to pull her rack off and dump a sack over her head and leave it there! She was a walking fun show and had no idea. Why hadn't she noticed what tops she was wearing? It wasn't as if she was wearing a low cut top that showed cleavage, which obviously would not be appropriate for work. She thought it was good to wear nice tight fitting tops to accentuate her body? She always chose tops that were bright and had gorgeous trims on them… this had gone all wrong.

Thankfully, she had a cardigan in her bag and quickly pulled it on, doing the buttons up to the top feeling the need to cover herself up. She shut down her computer and called out to her boss that she was on her way to see a client, and went downstairs to the cafe below to order a coffee. She needed to get out of that office fast and get some fresh air!

As she was waiting for her coffee she was thinking about the email again, the embarrassment of it all, her other colleagues in the office probably thought the same thing, but she didn't get how it was so bad when it wasn't showing skin. The guy called out her name for her coffee, she thanked him and headed out the front office door onto the main street. Her apartment wasn't too far from her work, so she decided she would walk home.

Fifteen minutes later she unlocked her front door and throwing her bag on the couch, she walked into her bedroom, took off her cardigan and looked at herself in the full length mirror, front on, then side on. And again turning even slower this time. Oh dear, ok… well she hadn't really stood and scrutinized what she had been wearing before. She had a black long pencil skirt on with a bright red high neck top that she had recently bought with cap sleeves. Her bust and the whole top of her looked MASSIVE, but how? What had happened, had it grown overnight? How had she not noticed it before? Then she turned side on… oh… holy mackerel that was just as bad.

She seriously looked like a lollipop, and this style is what she wore most days but just mixed it up a bit. Again thinking, as she was all covered, that it was appropriate. But now she could see how her bust was a focus. She didn't have a clue though what she could actually wear then, as if you are big on top, you are big on top, so what are you supposed to do? She can't go on like this, she had to be taken seriously, especially with the career she was going into. She didn't want to be a laughing stock. She wanted to be classy and respected.

She went over to her Dutch dresser and started opening all her drawers, pulling out top after top, and the skirts. None of it was any good, she would have to go shopping but she didn't know what to get. She had no confidence after this, that she would get it right. She was feeling stressed and upset.

One thing she was doing was calling in sick for tomorrow and maybe the next day too, she wasn't going back into that office until she had a plan in place. Just the thought of all this time, day after day, she had been doing it all wrong, she felt mortified. Tomorrow is a new day and it's all about me she says to herself.

NOW, what should Jayne have been wearing all this time? You will find out a little later…

Introducing Alice

She is in her early twenties and has a brown bob with a long fringe, cut dead straight sitting just above the eyes, which are brown. She is a solo mum with a young son called Caleb, aged five. She works full time as a marketing manager and her boyfriend James is a builder. They have been together for nearly two years. She lives in an outer city suburb.

Alice has the hourglass shape as we best know it.

This shape is all about those womanly curves! The bust and hips are well balanced and there is a beautifully defined waist (yes Mandy, I know!)

The upper body is proportionate in length to the legs, which are shapely. The waist is small in comparison to the hips, and bust.

The key is to proportionally dress the top and bottom, while accentuating the waist.

Let me tell you more after I have shared with you Alice's hurtful moment which led her to take the first steps in learning more about herself and her body to make some changes.

Alice was in her lunch hour and needing to find a new outfit for a dinner out with her work. It was a farewell to a lady who was leaving to move overseas. She picked up a cute dress, remembering again that dreaded day at work a few months earlier, it was still as clear as day and she wouldn't forget it in a hurry. Looking back now though, she is almost happy it did happen to wake her up about herself. But at the time it certainly took the winds out of her sails, that's for sure.

She was on the way to a scheduled appointment, but was busting, so quickly popped into the toilets on the way to the lift. She looked at her watch – yes she was ok for time. Alice had just closed the cubicle door when she heard a couple of girls come clip clopping in, their heels against the floor. By the sound of their voices, they were girls from her office, in reception. She listened again. Yes it was, it was Dana and Kate.

She was just about to call out hello to them when she heard her name. Or was it? She listened again, maybe she was hearing things? Just then she heard Kate say to Dana, 'can you believe how Alice is dressed today? Another awful outfit, I mean does she have NO idea at all, everyday it just gets worse and worse. It's a wonder she has a boyfriend… and he's really cute too… remember him at the last work party?'

'Oh yes… very cute!' Dana replied giggling.

Kate carried on. 'I wonder what he actually thinks of the way she dresses? I mean she looks like a big square brick… actually, that's what she reminds me of! One of those American footballers… you know with the big shoulder pads but like all the way down ha-ha'.

Alice felt herself go numb, in the distance she heard Dana say, 'oh I know… it's just SO wrong'.

Then the toilets flush, the doors open and shut, and as suddenly as they came in they were gone, and there she sat in the silence. She felt like she had just been whipped around by a tornado – completely dejected and morose. She quietly pulled her polka dot knickers up and pushed her pencil skirt down to where it sat on her hips and walked out to the mirror. She washed and dried her hands. She adjusted her jacket in the mirror. It was beige and straight cut, and met her skirt down on her hips. It was also beige and it was her fav box jacket, with the big shiny gold double breasted buttons she loved so dearly. She loved her gold.

Now though, she no longer loved it as dearly as she did half an hour ago. She wanted to take her whole outfit off and throw it in the bin, right then and there. Was she that unattractive that people talked about her like that? How did she not notice what she looked like? What did James also really think? Obviously, those girls thought he was far too cute to be with her.

Suddenly she remembered her scheduled meeting and looked at her watch.

'Oh,' she just didn't care anymore, promptly dialing the client's number she told him an emergency had come up, her apologies but she was now unable to meet with him today after all. She had once heard a funny quote that was perfect for her client today, a little smile on her face as she says out loud, 'today is not your day, and you are not the one'. Yes, that just about summed up her afternoon.

She got in the lift, hit the ground floor button, and headed out to her car park. The cool breeze hit her face. Stopping on the way to get a bag of donuts with extra sugar, and cinnamon, and a hot chocolate, just what she needed to comfort her hurt feelings.

Nearly colliding into an elderly lady as she made her way through the crowd and up the street. Eating her donuts and sipping on her drink, her mind not really on where she was actually walking, still hearing the girl's words repeating in her ear. As she walked past the shops, she looked at all the mannequins displaying all those pretty outfits. She would love to know what to buy and be able to just walk in, pull something off the rack, try it on, love it and buy it. Done! Just like that. Well, that was a joke that had never happened to her. Always zilch, zip, nothing. Maybe she wouldn't go in to work tomorrow either, just maybe she could come down with an awful virus. Yes, that would work. With a big deep breath in and out she reaches her sporty little red car and headed for home.

What should Alice have worn? Read that soon…

Lastly, meet Georgie

She is in her early forties, has short hair to the bottom of her neck in a pixie style cut with green eyes and a gorgeous smile. She is married to her high school sweetheart, Nathan. Georgie is a registered nurse at the city hospital where she has worked for the last ten years. Nathan is a physio therapist with his own business. They have been married for fifteen years, with no children.

Georgie's body shape is – The Pillar/Rectangle/Column.

This shape is generally taller and the shoulders, waist, and hips are similar sizes, and they have lovely long legs. So they need to show off their legs and arms.

They don't have broad shoulders but their bust is the same width as their slender hips. They don't have much in the way of a waist, tummy, and bottom. The shape is very much straight up and down. The only curves really being the bust.

The key to making the pillar look their best is to introduce shape, and emphasize curves. We will get into more detail about the shape later.

For now, Georgie's embarrassing moment. It was her turning point to learn about her body, how to dress it, and how to love it.

Georgie doesn't like fashion, she doesn't do pretty or girly, hasn't for a very long time. Well to be honest she doesn't really know how to, so maybe if she did, it would be a different story. One thing she is thankful for is that her friends are always telling her that she can eat whatever she likes and not put on an ounce. Apparently, she has a metabolism like a machine (so the doctor tells her), guess that's a bonus point.

Her friends have tried to dolly her up and make her over at times during the years but it just wasn't quite right and she felt uncomfortable. She knows Nathan would love it though if she did make more of an effort. She has also attempted to be more girly but just couldn't seem to pull it off, so she gave up.

It certainly had changed a lot after her encounter a little while ago. It is still a little humiliating to even think about, and she never told Nathan either what went down that night. This is what happened. She was in the supermarket one evening, doing the weekly food shop. She had her usual outfit on: straight cut grey pants and matching top, it was comfortable and practical. That's how she liked it, no fuss. She was half way through her shop and getting something off the shelf when she heard someone beside her say, 'Sir… excuse me sir'.

She carried on putting things in her trolley. She then felt a good tap on the shoulder, with a louder 'Sir! I don't know where to find the…' she turned around to see a lady whose face had gone quite blank, looking a little puzzled, and tripping over her words. She muttered, 'Oh… sorry… very sorry, I thought you were one of the men that worked here… oh I mean…oh'. Then quickly scurried away.

Ok, well that was interesting she thinks to herself, did the lady need glasses? I mean come on, yes I have short hair, ok I don't dress girly, but to be thought you were a man, which was a little harsh.

She kept pushing her trolley down the aisle, trying to put out of her mind what the lady had said. She turned the corner into the deli lane and then she stopped dead in her tracks. There was a long mirror against the wall of the columns in the lane. She saw a lady, this lady had short dark hair with a pixie cut. She kind of looked long and square all at once. All grey with a straight top and pants, the figure kind of looked like a box, no shape whatsoever. Really just like a clothes horse. Quite a manly looking clothes horse at that. But this lady was her.

Yes, she painfully admitted, yes she could be mistaken briefly for a man. That lady didn't need glasses; this is what she looked like. She started as someone brushed past her. She had stopped right in the middle of the lane. She quickly pushed her trolley over to the side. This brought back such horrid and painful memories of being teased relentlessly at school for looking like a boy – it all came flooding back. She didn't remember what she did next; did she just walk away from her trolley full of food?!....Yes she thinks she did. The next thing she knows she has pulled into her driveway at home and just sat there.

Her career was all about taking care of other people. She loved her job so much, she loved walking up and down the corridors of the hospital, her badge sitting proudly and her clock gently swinging as she walked, it was her other home. She had wanted to be a nurse since she was a little girl, apparently always dressing up and putting all her toys to bed, playing for hours bandaging them up.

Somehow and somewhere along the way she had lost herself. She felt that now she should care about what she looked like, for herself, for Nathan. It's not that she wanted to look and dress the way she did, she had tried in the past but it just didn't work. Then it became a habit and excuse, her work consumed her. Not anymore, it was time for her now.

With a new found energy she leaped out of the car and unlocked the front door and went quickly inside. Nathan looked up when she walked in, staring at her empty hands with a questioning look. 'Food is coming tomorrow now, it's all about me tonight!'

He looked at her blankly for a split second then says, 'ok babe… sounds great,' with an even bigger smile on his face.

Oh, how I love that man, she says to herself.

She threw open her closet doors and started pulling everything out and chucking it on a pile. Anything that looked like what she had on right then. She had to confess that was pretty much her whole closet.

'Out you goooo,' she says happily as she throws another top on the growing mound. She was feeling completely liberated.

What should Georgie have been wearing? Not long until you find out…

It was exciting times. I had recovered well with some much needed rest for my health. After my big decision of walking away from my corporate career to step back into the world of fashion and follow my heart (I had no idea what was ahead), everything was slowly coming together and on track for the first launch. I was very busy but it was not stressful for me. I was thoroughly enjoying every moment of building this "baby" and finally giving my own business time and energy, not someone else's. There is a quote I read the other day and it reminded me well of this exact time. It read "follow your dreams, or you will spend the rest of your life working for someone who did". So true, and a reminder to myself that I did make the right choice. Our launch date for the brand was set for December 1st and we were about ten weeks away from our deadline.

It was mid-week and I had gone to the shops to pick some things up. It was only about a ten minute drive from home. I was on my last errand and it was nearly time for the shops to close for the day. I pulled into the parking lot of a little block of shops. After finding a park, I jumped out and walked down the pavement toward the shop. As I was walking down the footpath, with the shops on my left and the car park on my right... out of the corner of my eye, I saw a car pulling into the space right in front of the pavement. I carried on a few more steps then glanced at it again as the speed caught my eye, it seemed to be moving fast. I was now directly in front of the car space the car was pulling into. It was a smallish black sporty looking car. I stopped this time, something wasn't right. So I turned around to face the park, then froze on the spot. To my complete horror, this car was coming straight at me! All I can remember of that terrifying moment was looking into the windscreen and seeing a lady with her mouth wide open. She must have been screaming as she was leaning over grabbing the wheel off the driver. It was a man, and he just had a blank, shocked look on his face. With a thud, I felt myself hit the bonnet of the car then go up in the air. Then blackness.

I came around with a lady bending over me, shaking me, quite hard. Asking me if I was OK. Initially, I thought, what is going on? Where am I? And why is this woman grabbing me?! She would have been in her fifties with light brown hair that was short and bouncy, dusted with some grey. She had lovely kind brown eyes. What was wrong with her though? She was looking so troubled. I looked around me, I seemed to be jammed up against the bottom concrete part of the wall of a shop, and on the ground. The lady was getting even more distressed and kept saying, 'they took off, they just took off, and I thought you were coming through my shop window with the car. Oh you are so lucky, are you OK? I'm calling an ambulance'.

Whoaaa, just hang on. She needs to stop talking for a second. They what? Who? Where? Everything was fuzzy, I was trying to get my mind in place but trying to do that just felt like I was wading through a deep fog.

She was talking so fast, I was trying to catch up on what she said. I say to her, 'It's OK, I am alright. Just let me sit here for a minute.' I was trying to comprehend what had happened, but I wasn't quite sure.

I looked down at my hands and saw they were shaking, and my neck and legs felt sore. Overall though, I thought I was alright. She said again, 'I'm going to call the ambulance you are in shock.'

I said, 'Please don't... I'm fine, I'm just going to go and sit in my car for a while.'

She then said, 'By the way I am Andrea'. Andrea then started to tell me what had happened, as she had seen it all from her shop counter.

'The car looked like it must have hit the accelerator not the brake, as it came fast into the park. It hit you then managed to stop before it went any further. I was terrified as I thought you and the car were going to come through the shop window. You just went up in the air and I don't know how you didn't go through the window. I ran straight out to you, and as I was checking you, I looked up to see the car racing out from the parking lot!'

There was no time for her to get the license plate number and Andrea said the shops and car park had no surveillance cameras. It was a couple in the car, and Andrea told me it was the lady leaning over, and grabbing the wheel and yelling something. That seemed to make the man slam on the brakes in the last moment. At the time I'm not sure how much of this I took in as I was still just trying to process everything. I told her I was going to go home, and again saying I would sit in my car first. She finally agreed and walked me over to my car, gently helped me in, and then told me she was shutting her shop early. She was going home now... to have a whiskey!

I sat in my car for I don't know how long then rung my husband Bevan, when he answered I just said, 'um... I was just hit by a car'. He yelled, 'What?! Where are you? Are you ok? What happened?' I repeated the events that Andrea had told me the best I could and what I could remember and he said, 'we need to call the ambulance and police right now'. I told him there was no point calling the police, we had no number plate of the car and there were no cameras, etc. I told him I was feeling a little sore but fine, and I wanted to go home. Reassuring him many times over that I was absolutely fine to drive, and that I would see him soon at home, he said, 'No, I'm coming to get you and take you to get checked out!' I told him I wasn't going anywhere (apparently I am rather stubborn) and that I would see him later. I promised I would call if I needed him.

So off I go, then as I come up to the lights, impulsively I turn in the other direction, deciding before I went home, I was well enough to go into another shop to try and get what I had originally come for. So I drove to the local mall.

Whilst there, I texted my daughter Lily-Rose and told her what had happened. She ordered me home straight away and couldn't believe that I was out shopping after what had happened. She was taking the "Mother Hen" role and told me I was treating it like it was no big deal. 'You've been hit by a car, go home Mum, now'. Oh dear. OK. She was sounding a little scary so I listened.

That night I was starting to feel worse and the pain started to escalate to another level I hadn't experienced. I didn't get much sleep. Daylight finally came and I remembered I had booked in a coffee date with a friend. I only just made it, sitting quite painfully as we had a catch up, then told her what had happened. I was actually pretty sore and going to take myself to the hospital. At this point, I was really starting to feel like I HAD been hit by a car.

Once again I headed off, at this stage, I was saying to myself, OK this just isn't the bruised pain that I had been thinking it was all night. This pain is getting worse with every movement of driving this car. I arrived, painfully got out of the car and walked very slowly to the building nearly buckling when I got inside the doors. One of the nurses saw me and straight away ran over to catch me telling me I was not looking so good. She took me to see the doctor immediately, and I had X-rays, the lady told me that it looked like a very badly bruised/sprained back. She did seem to spend some time looking at the X-rays though, and told me she wanted to get a second opinion. She couldn't right then though, as the person she needed wasn't due on until a little later. She sent me home, told me to put ice on it and rest.

A couple of hours later, while resting on my bed, I got the call. By this stage I was in complete agony and could barely move. They told me after a second opinion, that from my X-rays, my back was actually fractured and partly over the top of an old fracture. The old fracture they were talking about came from a horse riding accident many years before. So I had a stress fracture. Hello! That explained the pain, and of course all the driving that I had done, would have made it so much worse. My body had gone into shock, but I had been telling myself the whole time, to put my big girl panties on and deal with it. Like I usually do when something goes wrong.

The pain I felt that night was close to what I would describe as labor in my back. I knew all about that pain! Oh yes I do, as I had done that twice already in my life, having my two kids and naturally at that.

The thing is, I get anaphylactic shock, and get a severe reaction to any painkillers, not to mention a few other things. So I cannot take any allopathic medicine in any shape or form. I only take natural homeopathic medicine which pretty much saved my life when nothing else could. Oh, and did I mention that we were moving house the day after next? The timing of it all… sheesh. I mean it was really quite unbelievable. All the time at the back of my mind, was the launch. My precious "baby" was having its coming out party, and at this stage there was going to be no coming out at all.

We moved house as planned, with a lot of help from Mum and Dad of course. I will never forget the car ride. It felt like an eternity to reach the new house, it was about a half an hour drive away. Every bump and jar felt like I was being broken in two, whilst I clutched the sides of the seat until my fingers were white. Silently I looked out the window, away from Bevan so he couldn't see the tears of pain running down my face. Mentally telling myself to pull those big girl panties up even higher! I could do it, it would soon come to pass. These were always my mother's words whenever I was unwell.

She would always say that, 'Don't worry my darling, it will soon come to pass'. So I held onto that. With many years of on and off dreadful reactions, I had heard those words many times.

Back pain is so hard to describe to somebody who has not experienced it. As there is visually no blood coming out or bruises. It is hard for some people to understand just how horrific the pain can be. Bevan was driving as gently and smoothly as possible. Hands tight on the wheel, leaning over it, so he didn't miss a single thing. Looking out for any possible pot holes or a ridge in the road that would cause me further pain. When we were coming up to a tight bend or slowing down at the lights ready to stop, he would let me know, so I could prepare myself.

Finally, we arrive at the new house. The next step to deal with, was to get out of the car and get into the house. Of course, the master bedroom was located on the top floor. The things that I got myself into.

I was on total bed rest for about eight weeks. Let's just say I am not good at doing nothing, in case you haven't picked up by now. I am generally a pretty high energy type of person. I go mad not having things to do, I love being busy and having lots on the go. Almost to the point of verging on unmanageable. Yes, I do have issues, or else I guess one could just mention the word happy "workaholic". So I was complete doom and gloom with my order of bed rest. Bevan's cool and calm personality is an absolute bonus at times like these. If I am sitting there clucking like a hen, he calms me in a way I don't know how.

Back to the accident, which to our disbelief had been a hit and run. I was still getting my head around that. How anyone could actually hit someone with their car, see them go flying off the bonnet and hit the ground. Then see them lying motionless and just take off? Bevan, as I have already mentioned is a very chilled out person, but my accident would have to be one of the very few times I have seen him upset and angry. I must say, I thought about those people in that car many times when I was on my dreaded bed rest.

I always believed that in life everything happens for a reason. I am a positive person by nature and thought there has got to be a reason why this has happened. Good will come out of this, at some point, and right now I will just be eternally grateful that I am OK, and still have my legs. It could have been so much worse. There are many, many people out there, way worse off than little old me.

After my horse accident many years before, my kids were only little at the time – the horse I was trying out, to potentially buy, bolted on me in the middle of a cross country course at the local pony club. For those of you who don't know what "bolted" means on a horse, it is pretty much when a horse takes off out of the blue and does not listen to the stop signals. In other words, you have no control whatsoever and you just have to do your best to hang on. I was unable to hold my balance any longer, so I slid off the saddle to the side. My foot got caught in the stirrup iron and I couldn't get my foot out. I was then swung under the belly. The last thing I remember was feeling the legs push my body around. It was then that the big black tractor tire jump loomed up in front of me. Then all was black. To this day I cannot remember anything else of the accident. I was taken in the ambulance to the hospital and couldn't feel my legs for the first twenty-four hours. They wanted to operate and put a pin in my back but I refused. I told them I would do physio and everything else that it took, but I would not have surgery. Long story short, after many months, I recovered. I was left with back issues so I couldn't lift anything heavy or overdo it. It healed to some degree in time. The horse I was riding that day was called Romeo, I will never forget. He was so beautiful, part Arab and pure white. With the poshest tail you have ever seen, held up high, swishing from side to side, ever so proudly as he walked. I was always a sucker for beautiful horses. Well, after that I can tell you, I never looked at their beauty again. Romeo had definitely lost his Juliet, that's all I will say.

I was told by the doctors, that I shouldn't ride again as it was too dangerous. My back had been fractured in three places. That was pretty traumatizing. I just couldn't stop riding though, it was part of me, it was in my blood. I had been riding since I was about five years old. When I try and describe to Bevan how it feels to know I can't ride again, I tell him it is like him never been able to get in the water again and climb up on his board and ride the waves.

After that he got it, he has grown up at the beach and in the water, so for him not having water was like not having air. That is how I felt. When I was younger, and my friends were putting on makeup and going out with boys, I was at the paddock with gumboots on and dirt under my nails and picking up manure. My very first pony was called Charlie Brown. He was passed down to me by my sister. When she outgrew him I was the lucky new owner. He was chocolate brown, furry and loveable with a big gold nose. In our family we didn't have hand me down clothes, we had hand me down ponies! So some time after that first accident, I started my horse search again. Knowing I just couldn't and wasn't prepared to give up.

I eventually found the other love of my life – his name is Atlas. I knew from the moment I patted him, and when he rubbed me up and down my arm to say hello. Which really meant, I like you, please take me home with you. I did. I still have him now. He is my gentle giant, being a huge bay thoroughbred with the kindest eyes, the biggest hooves, the sweetest manner, and the biggest bottom lip you have ever seen on a horse. Apparently he didn't make the cut to race, as he was just too gentle, he didn't have it in him to hit the track. He was known when very young as the big boy with the big bottom lip. I have taught him how to kiss and he does it ever so beautifully. I just say, 'Give me a kiss Atlas' and he whacks his lips together clumsily against mine. He has such a sweet tooth so

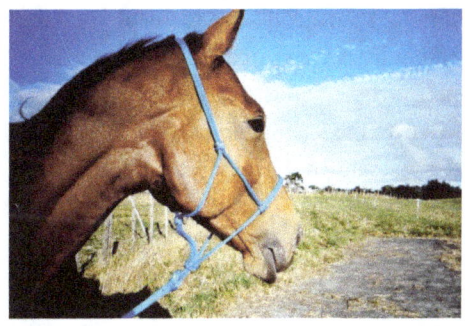

Atlas the gentle giant with the famous big lip.

every now and then I give him some carrots and apples dipped in molasses and he just goes crazy! Pulling the most hilarious faces. Total crackup to watch. He has been my therapy, he still is my therapy.

When I went through my divorce, he was there. I have galloped him through the forests laughing and I have plodded through them crying. He knew the days I was a little flat, as these were the day's he would rub me with his head and just keep rubbing longer than normal, coming in for a kiss. I will never forget the night I was at home. It was the evening in the summer so it was

One of the many funny faces.

He is a mummas boy and a real smoocher, taken before my accident.

still light outside. I had a gorgeous home with some acres of land. At this stage, my daughter had outgrown her first little pony and she was now very old, we kept her as couldn't bear to part with her. So she was retired. We also had my daughter's new pony. They would all graze just over the fence from the house. This day I had let them in around the house paddock to eat the grass down. I loved just being able to sit on the deck with them right there.

So this night, I was just sitting on the driveway, the concrete was still so lovely and warm from the hot day. Waiting for the sun to set. I was a little sad this night and had a few tears. Atlas was grazing not too far away, he walked over to where I was and stopped, still standing on the grass verge and not the concrete. I wasn't quite sure if I should jump up or not but couldn't be bothered anyway, so I just stayed put. Then I watched in complete amazement as this huge, strong beautiful animal got down on his knees right next to where I was on the concrete. He tucked his long legs under him and just sat there. As it was, I had only ever seen him from afar sitting, so for him to come over to me and park himself right next to me was something I could barely believe. I gently reached out and patted his face and his neck, not feeling alone as I had just moments before. I had an incredible bond with this horse, he knew me. He felt my pain. He sat there with me, for I don't know how long but when I got up after the sun had set, he did the same. The gentle giant clambering back up onto his feet, then just walked over to graze with the ponies. So many people under estimate these amazing animals... they get us. That horse has been through so much with me.

It was incredibly sad though, as after the hit and run accident. I was told again-no more riding. That if I rode and came off and knocked any prior injury, that I could be in a wheelchair for the rest of my life. It broke my heart, and I struggled so much with it. Watching everybody else saddle up and go for a ride. Oh how I missed tracking through the forest and along the beach, hooning up the hills and jumping over logs on the way. The smell of the leather, the feeling of sliding off his back after a great ride. I would say to myself, maybe if I just sat on him, maybe just a little ride, just down to the end of the paddock and back, surely that would be ok?

He is always up for a selfie.

NO, I would then battle back with myself. I had survived two broken backs and that was it. I was not a cat. I did not have nine lives. It was time to give it up. I sold my saddle before I had time to change my mind, as I knew if that was still sitting around I would be tempted. That was a good move as I have gone many times to put the saddle in the car and head out for a "little sit".

So now I just spend time with Atlas, grooming and feeding him, hanging out, he knows things have changed but he is great. We are happy to still just be together. The best of mates. We have awesome memories. He seriously gets spoiled rotten.

So there I was, we were launching the brand soon, and I was stuck in bed, flat on my back. The photo shoot had been done just the week before the accident, thank goodness, so that was one less major thing to worry about.

I used the time to do some study on marketing as well. Telling myself I should really make use of the time that had been forced upon me. I also started putting together some ideas and layouts for the new website. I learnt a lot in that time and also had lots of sketching time. Putting my pencil to paper again was an amazing feeling. With each sketch, I could see the clothes in my mind's eye, coming alive on the models. I could hear the rustling of the skirts and music beating loudly as their gorgeous heels thumped down the runway with attitude. The bold colors and print making such an impact. The accessories perfectly cohesive with the look… I could see it all.

After all that, the first of December rolled around and we launched on time, and unbelievably, Lilika Designs was born. She finally got her coming out party. It was a great success. Within half an hour of the website going live we had our very first order. Then they kept coming. I was super proud that through all the challenges, I had achieved my goal. I was now living inside my world of color that I had been craving for many years. I could officially say, 'See you later!' to that stiff, unfriendly world of black and white.

A snap of me back doing what I love- playing with fabric.

About six weeks later, I was contacted and told I had been chosen along with fifteen other emerging designers worldwide to showcase my brand in Manhattan NYC. YES, I was in shock. Of course, I had just got back into the industry after years of being away. To be invited to something like this was absolutely amazing. Then I saw the date of the show. Shut uppppp…. it was in seven weeks. I read through all the information. It stated I had to take a "look" book and press kit with me for meeting with media. Wow, this was too much too soon. The collection I was to show had to be a new collection, a one off couture collection. OH MY.

My initial thought was there is no way, I can't do this, how will it work? There is no time to plan. I am in New Zealand, it is in New York. There was so many things running through my mind all at once to think about. But no time. I needed designs, I needed fabric, I needed samples, I needed to do a photo shoot, find a model, find a photographer, my mind was scrambled. Argggh. I went back and forth for the next couple of days, leaning towards passing up on the opportunity, then totally excited and ready to charge back on it.

Both my kids kept telling me, 'You have got to do this, this is an amazing opportunity. Lilika will be out there on an international level, even before a national level. This is your time, just do it Mum'. I must have done something right with them. They are the most gorgeous human beings, and I am blessed to have a special bond with the both of them. I stopped and thought, how many times have I told them, 'You can do anything in life, just follow your heart, take a step at a time and grab every opportunity that comes your way'? LOTS of times. It was time to practice what I preach, and so made the call… yes I am going!

My mum, dad and hubby are my other biggest supporters, they were so happy for me. Hang on though, I couldn't go alone. I wanted to share this with someone, besides I would need assistance with the show. Mum was not a good flyer so that was out of the question, but oh… there was one person that I knew would be up for any adventure. She had already been telling me to make this happen. She lived for it, any excitement that came her way and she was in the middle of it. She also happened to be an amazing hair and makeup artist, having done my hair and makeup for nearly twenty years, along with being one of my dearest friends, Sheryl. She would be the best person to share this with. She has traveled all over the world chaperoning girls to pageants, doing their styling for them. She loves fashion, and like me, loves anything shiny; we are a couple of magpies when together.

I rung her up and asked her if she would come with me. After the initial screams of excitement, nearly deafening me on the phone, yes, yes, yes. We made our plans and within the next week our flights and hotel were booked. We were officially confirmed for the show. Hooray!

The chicken dance began. It was now only six weeks until the show, thanks to my time of bed rest (my silver lining), I already had some of my sketchbook pages filled with designs. I shopped until I dropped, sourcing and finding the fabrics I wanted over the next few weeks. I found a great model, and a photographer, plus hair and makeup. As soon as the samples were done, we carried out the shoot. It is amazing what you can do when you put your mind to it. We had the pleasure of being offered a beautiful country mansion which was the perfect location. I knew from the start what I wanted for the "look" book… to not just have shots against a white wall like just about everyone else does. Instead, to showcase our beautiful Kiwi backdrop. The lovely lady who offered us her home later became a great friend. Her name is Jing.

Jing is an amazing business woman and an inspiration on all that she has achieved. I asked her one day when I was fitting for a dress that she would wear in London to accept her second major international trophy for her best Pinot Noir (she is a wine maker). Her business is called

Crown Range Cellar. Jing was telling me her story of how it all began for her. I asked her what advice she would give to someone to have a successful business. She said one word to me. "Resiliance."

That made me feel pretty good as that was definately something I felt I already had under my belt. Be resiliant.

As busy as we both are, we always make the time for each other amongst crazy schedules to have a coffee/brainstorming catchup. These are always incredibly fun times with highly motivated thinking, ideas and planning flying around for both our business and how we can work together.

We are always so charged up like we have literally been plugged into an electric socket for the last twenty-four hours! We totally feed off each other's energy, excite-

Jing and I at one of our catch ups.

ment and drive with what we are doing. I truly believe it is because we are both living our dream life. We wake up and get to do what rocks our boat every single day, we are in charge of our own business and in turn this drives and builds our amazing life.

In your life time there are very few people that you will meet that are literally living their passion every day. That have built a wonderful life for themselves out of hard work, determination, persistence and a pure happiness for what they do. We are on the same wave length, nothing is too big or too far out of reach for either of us. If someone was to watch our meetings they would think we were mad or they would want what we were drinking! Every now and then we jump up and clap our hands together in a high five, from some new idea that has just come to life. You see, what I have learnt through my journey is that successful people are only ever happy for you and supportive, they never question your dreams; they get excited for you. They share the feeling of success with you. They do this cause they know what it feels like, they are confident in their own skin and where they are going in life. The opposite to the naysayers I have already talked about in this book, who will try to bring you down, the successful ones you will find, only lift you up.

Jing and I have great respect and affection for one another, and I love being around like minded people who just 'get you'.

I am blessed enough to have some very special and amazing relationships, personal and business in my life. You will hear a little later about Natalie, she is another wonderful, inspirational and successful woman.

Passion, Fashion & Heart

From the moment Lilika was born. I was determined for "her" to be different, to be full of life, energy, personality, and color. To also be a bit cheeky and playful. She was to be posh, designed for women who wanted to stand out – not just fit in.

The photo shoot was a great success. Of course being my first one for a very long time, I was a little rough around the edges. Thankfully, I had a great team around me. I learnt a lot from that first shoot and the next one was very different. Time was now running out though, there were only a few days to go. On the day we were due to leave for the airport, I was still getting it all ready.

One of the shots taken inside at the photo shoot (not knowing at the time this photo would end up inside the pages of a glossy US Fashion magazine with a full page feature)

We had allowed ourselves a full day after reaching the US, to finish any work and final touches for the show. My mother had been madly pressing all the garments and working with me tirelessly to bring it all together. Once more they were special times, with always so many giggles along the way. We had made it happen. I knew my grandmother would have been so proud of us. As we would work Mum would recall snippets of memories of her mother and tell me some stories. Her memories, of course, were not that many, she was only seven and unfortunately, our minds seem to bank the bad memories more than the good. They are so traumatic and profound they just stick with us, don't they? Not long after she lost her mother, her grandma also died. Her grandma was her other mother, who she loved so dearly. Such huge loss for such a little girl. She told me that after my grandmother died, she found in her room a half finished dress she had been working on. She so vividly remembers the fabric and the style, even the feel of the fabric. Another dress she actually remembers her wearing was a blue polka dot one. So one day we saw some beautiful blue polka dot fabric and got it for her. Mother made a dress for herself in it. I think these things just bring her closer to her.

That's why I really believe her being a part of Lilika, brings her memories back to life. The next collection I was to make, I named our favorite frock the "Manoula", after grandma, which means mother in Greek. I often call Mum that. It was so popular too. Recently, we decided that we would make mother a dress like the one grandma never got to finish as she can remember the fabric so clearly. Now… back to the trip.

Outside shot on location.

Bevan drove me to the airport which was about an hour from where we lived. We met Sheryl there. We checked in with the precious cargo, like excited school children, on their first camp. Looking like we had packed pretty much everything but the kitchen sink, we were of course over our weight limit. So we were swapping and stuffing things back and forth, all over the place until we had the weight right. The lady at check-in told us there was a change with the flights and instead of stopping over at Brisbane we would be stopping at Sydney instead. OK, well that didn't seem like an issue.

We said our goodbyes to the guys (both the hubbys) and went through the departure lounge. Going through the walk through customs area, you show the machine your passport. Then you go through the little gate, get your photo taken, and then go out through the other side. Should be easy right? Well, I had got through and Sheryl was in the one beside me. When I reached the other side, I hear my name being called out. I turn around and there is Sheryl. I don't know how but she is stuck inside the little gates yelling at me, 'I can't get out, I can't get out'. She hadn't taken her carry on case through with her, so it was on the outside.

She was trying to get back out to get it but of course the gate locks once you go through. Oh my goodness, we hadn't even left NZ yet. It was always fun times with this lady, I can tell you that. I watch as she then tries to actually climb back over the gate to get back to her bag. I started yelling out to her, 'Sheryl, no you can't do that, just wait, I will get someone to help you'. I go and grab one of the officers and ask for some help.

He takes one look at her and says, 'What IS that woman doing?' Oh dear, it was a little embarrassing. He goes over and gets it all under control. Gets her out, gets her bag and steps her slowly through the process the right way. That over with, we sit down and have a drink and something to eat. I was so looking forward to getting on the plane. It had been a manic few weeks. I had been up the majority of the night before, like many others over that time, and had a bit of a headache. Several hours of sleep on the plane would do the trick. Famous last words. That was not to be. I could not sleep, and trying not to think of our twenty-seven hour flight ahead of us, I told myself all would be well and I would just have a big sleep from Sydney through to LA.

Sheryl was full of energy, as usual, a box of jumping beans. I thought, well, if I wasn't going to sleep, it was the perfect time to unveil the look book to her. I had not told her a thing so she had no idea, and had been waiting ever so patiently (especially for her) and with great anticipation to see the designs. To see what I had been crazily working on for the last six weeks. She loved the collection and just kept raving about it, I was so happy for the positive feedback, even if she was possibly a little biased. She is always very straight up with me. We had so much to catch up on and chatted the rest of the way, and I dare say, driving the people in the seats behind us slightly mad. They would have been thankful for their earplugs.

We were told in NZ we would have a stopover for three hours and then catch our connecting flight through to the US. Easy peasy. After touchdown in Sydney, we went through to the international connecting desk, happily chatting away, pleased to be stretching our legs again. The lady checks mine, all good, checks Sheryl's, checks again, looks at her watch then at Sheryl. Then back down at her passport… finally looks up at Sheryl.

'Your esta (visa that allows you entry through to the States) does not match your passport details, so it is not valid. As this is a connecting flight through to the US this must be in order here. You need to apply for a new one before you can depart. Your connecting flight through to Los Angeles leaves in twenty-five minutes.'

Just like that. In a very matter of fact tone, totally dropping an already exploding bomb. Ah-hhhh….We look at each other in complete shock, twenty-five minutes?! What happened to three hours and apply for a whole new visa? Whaaaat!

We were just standing there, like stunned mullets. The pair of us. I can feel my temples start to throb a little more intensely. Like little wee hammers, bang, bang, bang. We were rooted, just rooted to the spot.

She must have seen the shock on our faces and says, 'look, you need to get upstairs fast and use one of our airport computers, get on the website, and apply for the new visa. Get the reference number then come back to me. It won't take you long, and you should still make your flight'.

Without a word, we turn around and just run. We run along to the elevators, (remember I am in heels whilst I am hooning through this airport), we run up the elevators with me yelling to Sheryl, 'get all your info out ready for the website so I can jump straight onto the site and start the applica-

Selfie with Sheryl on the plane, the first leg of the journey.

tion… and run, run faster lady!' 'Run forest, run!' came to my mind. Oh, if it hadn't been so stressful it would have been funny.

We get to the floor, skid to a stop and see the computers. They are all busy, are you kidding meeee? Someone get off please, I silently pray. Please, please, we need to get on.

A few minutes later one is free. I jump on, hands shaking, typing in the web address. Why is it when you know you need to go fast you seem to do the opposite? It is like when you have an awful dream and someone is chasing you, and you are in slow motion and just can't go fast. Yeah, that. That's what it felt like. I call out the questions to Sheryl, she gives me the answers to put in the boxes.

We come to the last page but her parent's details section just won't go through. I keep saying, 'are you sure that's right? It's not letting us through to the final page'. Then the page times out, and I have to start all over again! At this point my stress levels are at an all time high, the little hammers are now not so little any longer, my head is throbbing badly.

Then to top it all off, our names are now getting called out over the loud speaker, 'final call, final call for passengers….'. It is now my third attempt and we can't get past this page, and once again it times out. Completely exasperated and frustrated, with my patience now thinning to a very fine thread of cotton. I hear another speaker call. I say to Sheryl, 'Quick, we need to get back to the lady at the desk downstairs, and tell her we are having issues and can't finish the application'. We grab our bags and run back downstairs again like mad women through the airport. People stopping and staring at us. We catch the lady as she is walking away from the desk. Telling her, with words tumbling out rapidly what's happened. Sheryl and I are almost in tears at this point.

She says, 'Come with me I will take you to the gate'. She had softened with our obvious distressing plight. A little glimmer of hope that we can sort this out.

Our names are still being called as we race up to the gate, she tells them what has happened. The ladies at the desk are not impressed and openly unfriendly.

One lovely lady comes up to us from behind and says, 'let me quickly get on my phone and see if I can get us through the application. Maybe it's just our computers.'

The manager at the gate says to her, 'You have exactly five minutes, I am not holding this plane any longer.' That is one grumpy lady. Maybe it is close to her coffee break.

Sheryl promptly bursts into tears saying, 'What are we going to do?!' Meanwhile, the lovely lady is clicking on her phone as fast as her fingers will allow her. Asking us the questions as she goes. She gets to the same page with the parent's details and can't get though either.

She says, 'I am so sorry I can't do it.'

Just then the lady at the gate comes up to me and says, 'Right that's it, time's up, this plane is going. As your Esta is in correct order, you can get on the plane now and go through to LA. You will have to go alone or you can stay here with your friend'. My head pain is now so bad I can barely function and start to feel sick.

My mind is racing, all the last six weeks to make this happen and now it is all gone just like that, the show, everything I had worked for. But I cannot, and will not go ahead without my friend. We are in this together. The lovely lady grabs our hands and says, 'Look… I will make some calls and see what flights are available, we will try get you through to NYC as soon as we can.'

The gate lady is now almost yelling at me, 'Are you going or staying?!'

I say quietly, 'I am staying.'

She rolls her eyes and yells out to one of the crew waiting, 'Get their bags off now and shut the doors.'

Sheryl goes off with the lady who takes her through to the Esta office to apply for a new one. She was told that the problem was, when it came to the parent's section, that we were putting in the married name, not the maiden name. Sheesh, I mean what are the chances.

Meanwhile, I had told them to just park me up at McDonald's while they did that. All I could think about was sitting still, and I had gotten a sudden craving for some McDonald's salty fries. I always tend to feel like really salty things when not feeling well, it almost wasn't a good sign I wanted the fries.

After the new Esta has been processed and Sheryl had all her papers in order, we go back to the lounge area. The lovely lady makes some calls, and I sit down in a very fragile state, not believing what happened. I can't move for the pain in my head, it has now turned into a migraine and I need to get to a bed, to lay horizontal ASAP. I have already had to run to the bathroom to be sick once. Amy, the lovely lady, we finally took notice of her name tag, says with a big smile, 'I have managed to get you flights through to LA, first thing tomorrow morning!'

We hug and thank her, we can still make the show! We will be arriving the night before though, and late, but who cares. We will be there in time. The relief I feel, oh, ouch, the little hammers I feel.

Amy rings and books us into a hotel for the night, and then calls us a taxi. She has gone above and beyond, and really pulled it all together for us again. Bless her. After a horrific bumpy ride in the taxi, as there were roadworks in the direction we were headed… Of course, why should it be a smooth ride at this point in the game. I can't even speak, we check in and go up to our room. I had double vision on and off at this point.

I climbed in between the gorgeous luxurious bed sheets, buried myself under the covers and just cried with the stress and pain of it all. But that did not help.

Sheryl, at this stage, was feeling dreadful. She explained what had happened. After she had applied and received her Esta, her son suggested that as her passport was getting close to expiry that she should get a new one, to be safe. So she did, of course forgetting that she now had a new passport with a new number. The Esta she had now did not have the same details. It was what it was, and it was done, we just needed to move forward now and make the trip happen.

As I am just trying to get off to sleep all of a sudden Sheryl leaps off the bed next to mine and yells, 'The limo, the limo!' I look at her thinking OK, she has officially lost it. Great. We aren't even there yet. She says again, 'I need to cancel the limo they will be waiting for us at JFK, and we won't be there!'

Give me strength, thinks I.

She starts pulling a thousand bits of paper out of her bag. Then again she yells out, 'Oh no, the hotel, the hotel too!' Not even able to speak. I think to myself, she is going to have to take care of this one for me. I am completely unable to manage anything else. I gently lay my head back on the soft feather-filled pillow and start counting with each hammer of pain in my temples. I will count them, just like people count sheep. Oh dear, and you think Sheryl has lost the plot.

Sheryl messaged my daughter Lily-Rose for me, as on top of everything else my phone was not working outside the country. Even though it had been set up to do so. It was so awful not being able to contact Bevan and tell him what was happening. He is my rock in those moments and I was missing him so much already. Sheryl told Lily-Rose we were in Sydney overnight, not heading to LA as we should be.

I barely slept all night and we had to be at the airport early again.

Sheryl wanted us to have a fun and comfortable ride into our hotel when we arrived in the States. Hence the booked limousine. Bless her, she was all for the fun. Thankfully, she had got hold of the company just in time and they re-scheduled our pick up. The same for the hotel. Before we leave I suggested that we take a photo on the balcony. Even though it had been a rough ride so far I wanted to build the memories. So we ask the bellboy when he collects our bags to take the shot… Sheesh I was feeling like I had just been steam rollered.

But finally, we checked in, went through customs and boarded the plane for LA and our final flight through to JFK. Just happy to be on a plane and finally heading towards our destination, we tried to enjoy the ride. I still had a bad headache, although better than the day before. I was unable to sleep. Meanwhile, Sheryl was tucking into the food along with numerous hot chocolates, and having the time of her life. I had never seen her drink so much hot chocolate, it was either incredibly amazing, or the cute and friendly guy with the dimples delivering them may have had something to do with it.

This is why she is with me, she always makes the best of every situation, good or bad. I was still not up to eating at this point, as I was still feeling a little nauseous with the pain.

There was a girl next to Sheryl on the other side who started talking to her and asking her what we were doing and where we were going. Sheryl could barely get a word in, answering one rapid question after the other. I just listened quietly. Then the girl says to Sheryl that she believes Sheryl is her sister! That this is a trip they have done together before. I heard that part and tried to smother a giggle.

Early morning photo on the balcony of our Sydney hotel.

Sheryl slowly turns to look at me, with an elbow hitting my arm and a raise of her eyebrows. Along with a "help me!" look in her eye. Ha-ha… oh this is so funny. I am so pleased I am on the other side and try not to laugh out loud. This went on for some time and Sheryl politely keeps talking to her new "long lost sister".

To stop the girl talking, she all of a sudden says to me, 'Oh we must get a selfie, we haven't got one yet on the plane'. So we shift close together, then just as I click the button we see a face shoot into the frame. Well, if that wasn't a photo bomb I don't know what is. Ha-ha the "sister" had also wanted to be a part of the shot. After that, Sheryl quickly got out her earplugs and shoved them in and faced my direction to avoid any eye contact.

We ended up having a smooth connecting flight from LA through to JFK, both pretty exhausted at this point after twenty-seven hours of flying. I had not slept a wink on any of the flights. Not one single shut-eye. It didn't help having the time to just sit there, and think of all the different things that needed to be done before the show still. Just switch off. I whispered to myself. Turn your mind off! Yeah-nuh, that was not going to happen in a hurry.

We arrived at JFK, get our luggage and go through to the front doors. After Sheryl spent about ten minutes trying to figure out the suitcase trolleys were locked, and you had to pay, unlike NZ (we so must have looked like a couple of country bumpkins). She heaves our massive load of cases onto the trolley, stacked so high she could barely see where she was going. We walk into the arrivals lounge and find a guy holding a board with our names on it. We follow him over to the undercover carpark area. There sits our gigantic big black shiny limo. Sleek and magnificent.

I can't believe this limo is just for the two of us, it is massive inside. We both stretch out in luxury ready to fall asleep, but both trying so hard to stay awake, and enjoy the ride into the city. Neither of us says it but we know all we are thinking about is the day we have lost, that the show is in the morning and we have a ton of finishing work yet to do.

The limo guy asked us a couple of times, 'Do you want some music on? Have some fun for your first time to NYC.'

We looked at him with a tired smile and said, 'No music thanks, we just want to rest.' He looked at us like we were plain weird, and then didn't say another word for the rest of the ride.

We see the city skyline for the first time and with a new found energy and excitement, we leap up out of our seats, grab our cameras and like true tourists, snap away at everything in sight. Coming over the bridge into Manhattan was just so beautiful. At this point, all I could see of Sheryl was her butt, as she was literally hanging out the window taking shots.

We arrived outside our hotel after about an hour. Sheryl always one for a photo opportunity, asks the limo driver for a photo. We pose in front of the limo with the bustling city streets behind us. I couldn't believe we were there. On the streets of NYC for the first time.

We checked into our gorgeous room, collapsing on our beds for the next half an hour, big sighs escaping was all that could be heard.

All of a sudden we realized we were hungry, dialled room service and ordered a big plate of food (which, by the way, was one of the best gourmet pizzas I have ever tried) with thick salty fries- it was heaven. You will get to realize that I just adore fries, when I'm well, when I am sick, just feed me fries and I am a happy camper. They are seriously my weakness.

We start unpacking the collection. There is still so much to do, it's now nearly midnight and we are about to start work. My headache is now just down to an ache and had thankfully moved out of the dysfunc-

Our fab Limo

tional migraine, hammering stage. It had come to pass.

We are here, we made it in time and the show we have planned for is tomorrow. I feel the excitement building. I pull out the first design and try it on for Sheryl, falling in love with my creation all over again.

One by one I tried them on with all the accessories, clip clopping around in stilettos. Sheryl oohing and ahhing at them all, then once the mini fashion show was over, I bagged them ready for tomorrow, whilst

Finally on our way to Manhattan

thinking of my precious mother who had sat there and sewed all the buttons. I was so blessed to have been given a mother like her. Then I look up and there was the lady, my dear friend. Propped up in amongst all the pillows, glasses on, needle and thread in hand working away on some amendments. I felt so thankful to have her in my life, a true friend who will literally do anything for me. It was now three in the morning and we stopped for a cuppa.

We still had a couple of hours of stuff to do but were completely shattered. The extra sugar in our drinks had not lasted long at all.

I am just going to rest for a moment I think until I hear a noise, what is that? I hear some more, is that a horn? No can't be, I sit bolt upright, it's daylight, those are horns beeping, where am I? OH NO… I turn to the other bed. Sheryl is fast asleep a garment she was working on still in her hand. I yell out at her, 'Quick, get up, we fell asleep!!!' I have never seen her move so fast. That woman literally woke up and catapulted out of that bed like a ball out of a canyon. Oh dear, maybe I shouldn't have yelled like that quite so loud.

Glimpse of the skyline heading over the bridge.

Yay the super jet lagged Kiwis made it, taken outside our hotel.

I am too scared to look at the time, but do. It is eight am. Are you kidding me? How could this have happened? We need to leave for the show at nine and we haven't finished our work, or got ready. Thankfully, we both knew what we were wearing so it was just hair and makeup to do. Sheryl starts laying out the makeup and tells me to sit down while she gets the big bottle of hairspray out.

You see, I have been given the gift of big, curly, uncontrollable hair that needs to be tamed. The kind that when you go for a holiday in the islands (yes the air is humid there but still). Hair that when you put the straighteners through does nothing and just poofs up.

Yeah, you got me now right? Anyway, so the bottle of spray comes out and she does her magic. I just go with it now, I no longer fight my hair. I have learnt over the years to just embrace it. I can be the designer with a birds nest on top of my head. At least I shall be remembered.

As soon as my hair and makeup are done, oh that is what is so fabulous about having a friend who has had many years in the industry. You don't have to worry about trying to attempt it yourself. I trust my face and my hair to her, like my life. Not many people get to go near my hair after having it hacked off. Without realizing what was actually happening, I cried all the way home. I have always had long hair, since a little girl. I realized just how much I loved it when I lost it. That is was also a bit of a security blanket. Hubby nicknamed me 'Bichon' not long after we met. Think you now get the full picture of my hair.

While Sheryl throws her clothes on, then starts on her own hair and makeup, I start gently packing the collection into the suitcases, thankful that each look had been bagged the night before, or should I say early this morning. There is so much to take, we have a huge case just full of shoes. I must admit, shopping for all the accessories was a pure delight. My favorite thing "putting the icing on the cake" is the final styling. Love it. Checking what we have left to do, which now will have to be finished when we get there.

I ring downstairs for the bellboy to come up and collect our bags for nine am. It is eight forty. We hadn't had breakfast or anything. Oh well, too bad, no time, our precious three hours sleep had really screwed up our timing, but at least we had got some sleep. Then it dawned on me, hallelujah, my headache had gone. Hooray for no pain. Yay for no little hammers pushing me to the brink of insanity.

Sheryl started work again on the last few things until the bellboy arrived. I needed to look up where we were going – when I had looked back at home it said it was only about a fifteen minute drive. It had got to ten past nine and still no bellboy. I rang the lobby again. They apologized saying they have been so busy all morning. Someone will be right up. Right, OK. Waiting, waiting, another ten minutes went past and nothing. That's it, we decided we would just haul all the suitcases down ourselves. We couldn't waste any more time. Poor Sheryl, the whole way on the trip, she had been taking the brunt of all the heavy stuff.

After my accident, my back couldn't cope with much. The last thing we needed was that seizing up. One thing I can tell you though, is there is no way I was NOT wearing my heels. Since my back got better, everyone told me, oh you can't wear heels anymore. You will have to go with flats. Yeah… Nuh! I have given up my horse riding, and I ain't also giving up my heels. I will be buried in them I can tell you that much. Preferably ones with a pop of pink. Maybe with a tincy bit of bling.

We swipe our room locked and make our way to the lift down the hallway. Sheryl's shoulder bag she had put over the handle of her carry on case, kept swinging off every two minutes and whacking her on the back of her legs. The next time, it got her right in the weak point at the back of the knees and it buckled on her, causing her to almost summersault over the big case she was lugging. It was so funny, I got the giggles and couldn't stop. She then started up. Oh dear, we could barely walk straight we were in hysterics.

She was saying to me, 'Stop it, stop it our makeup will run and we'll look like freaks!' Everything had caught up with us along with our newly adorned, nervous energy for the show. Now, it was also looking like we were going to be late.

We stumble into the lift still laughing, barely fitting in with all our cases and as the doors close we see the bellboy arrive and walk toward our door – a bit late now dude. We Kiwi girls get stuff done!

The lift door lets out a pretty little ding, opens up and we fly out. In the lobby we ask at the concierge desk to call us a taxi ASAP. The lady at the desk said, 'I can do that but I don't know how long they will take to get here, you may have to wait about fifteen minutes.'

Whaaaat? It was now ten to ten, we had to be at the show location at ten.

It will be fine I say, all good, no worries at all. Keeping up our, 'She'll be right mate' Kiwi attitude. If we are a little late we are a little late, we have done everything in our power to make this happen. From missed planes, migraine, no sleep and currently no food, we can hang in there a little longer. Meanwhile, as we are waiting I catch Sheryl looking at the gift shop in the corner. I say to her, 'lady don't you even think about it!' She is dying to go into the gift shop, I can see from now, she is going to need a suitcase just for the shopping there, let alone anywhere else.

We were both starving. I normally have my coffee every morning and early. I hadn't had a thing, so I was just hanging out for a gulp of what Sheryl calls my "tar". I drink black coffee. The only way to drink it I say. Must be the Greek coming out. As that's exactly how they drink it. Mum was brought up from a very young age, on what they call "Briki" which is a very strong and very small coffee. It looks like an espresso shot but it is to be sipped. Greeks love their coffee and it is quite a serious social affair that can go for hours! But I don't have that time right now to be drinking like a Greek girl.

The taxi arrives! Hooray, we tell him that we are going to the garment district, and he says, 'Don't worry I will get you there as fast as I can.'

We sink back into the seat and look at each other and smile, we are on our way. I don't have a clue what I look like, as I chucked my outfit on after my hair and makeup was done and ran out the door. If only people knew. They probably thought we both took hours of primping and preening ourselves ready. Oh no. For how we were looking on no sleep at all in the last forty-eight hours, and such a short time to get ready, we were not looking bad at all.

We take some photos in the back seat and look out at the amazing majestic skyscrapers surrounding us. NYC with hundreds of beeping yellow taxis. I was in love! The energy of it, the beauty of it, and the manic feel was just amazing. It does something to you, I had heard people say that before, now I got it.

As promised, the taxi driver pulled up right outside the location. We are only ten minutes late so not bad at all. I jump out of the taxi. All I see is black and grey clothes and some more black and grey clothes, and all these faces looking at us. I look down at my hot pink and electric blue outfit, my high-low skirt with my lace crop top. To complete the look, my favorite pair of super high Steve Madden wedges. That is what I later called "my legally blonde" moment. I could only picture what they were seeing. This big mop of blonde curly hair and bright colors, like they have probably never seen before, all in one outfit. Then I look over at Sheryl, all dollied up in her super classy black and cream lace dress with strappy black stilettos and bling accessories. She really did look rather gorgeous. OH MY. Were we out of place, or were we out of place. Yip…. we were out of place!

I turn to Lady and say (that is her nickname), 'Um... I don't know about this... what am I doing? I haven't done this in years and years, and here I am about to show in Manhattan. I am feeling so out of my depth here all of a sudden.'

She replies, 'Come on girl, none of that. This is what you came for and you are going to blow them away with who you are, and what you have created'.

Oh, how I love this woman. So we haul our cases up to the front door and with what feels like a thousand eyes on us, we try to stand and wait like we don't have a care in the world. Like we just rocked on up here, had days of rest and relaxation, and of course total organization. Like we are just black and grey like the rest of them. Sheryl strikes up a conversation with a mother and daughter from the UK, who are lovely. So we chat away with them. Faye, the organizer arrives just then and opens up the doors. We all scuttle in and hop into the lift.

One of the other designers gives me a bit of a once over and says, 'so what is that accent, where are you from?' 'New Zealand,' I say proudly. She promptly rolls her eyes and laughs, 'Oh you must be pleased to get out of there.'

Sheryl gives me the elbow (you will get to see that she does this quite often) and a little too sharply, ow that hurt. Um, I think to myself, no not really, I love NZ... actually. Anyway each to their own, then the lift doors open and out we go. The building was beautiful, we were on the top floor. Stunning high ceilings, white walls and blonde wood floors. It was a fabulous space. Welcome to Manhattan, I say to myself.

Let me just confess, we had no idea what to expect. I had been out of the industry for so long, so this whole experience was totally new and completely out of my comfort zone. A lot had changed over the years. Let's not forget I had only launched the brand six weeks earlier.

On the way to the show.

As we unpacked the collection and hung it up carefully, one by one, on our given rack, I had a couple of designers come over and ask to look at the collection. One didn't say anything after flicking her way through, the other said, she loved the color. She then said to me, 'I just love the outfit you are wearing, did you design it? Did you do it especially to go with your collection?'

I said yes I had and thanked her. Thinking, well of course, it was Lilika! She had a cute dress on, I could see her collection hanging just behind her, the colors looked similar.

I said, 'Your dress is super cute, is it one of yours?' Why did I ask that? It was a stupid question, of course it's hers, and she is a designer. She had just asked me the same thing about Lilika and I had scoffed at that!

She then surprisingly answers, 'Oh no, this isn't my design, it's just a shop bought one'. I was gobsmacked and surprised she wasn't wearing her own clothes. I mean, it is such an amazing opportunity to wear your own brand at any time, especially when you are showcasing in NYC. I got that a lot though over the day, the media asked me the same thing, stating how much they loved it. I had decided at home that I wanted to wear something from the collection... but make it a little different, so I could show off another whole design on the runway, during the finale walk, and still be cohesive within the collection.

Getting side tracked for a moment – after I got back to NZ from the show I was asked to speak at the Auckland University Business School, to lecture on how I built my brand from the ground up and the steps I took to make it a success (by the way, another first for me in public speaking). I had a wonderful class of entrepreneurs. I told them this story as an example of how I was blown away that a designer would not walk down the runway in her own design… Back to the show…

The collection was now hanging in order on the rack. It looked gorgeous. The hot pinks, the bright blues, the pretty florals and the blocks of white, not to mention the 'to die for' delicate lace. What was once in my mind, then on a pencil sketch, was hanging before me. That sketch was now filled in with bold color and print with perfect lines and structure. All the detail added with trims and delicate buttons. I loved it all.

The looks were all numbered with their shoes and accessories, set out ready to go. I was kind of hoping that I would be later in the runway order so we had time to finish our bits we still had to do. I was starting to feel a little apprehensive. Suddenly the organizer Faye calls out, 'right here come all the models, you have twenty minutes to fit them, once the twenty minutes are up that's it. The models will then move on to the next designer, so choose wisely and quickly as this is your only chance'.

I am stuck to the spot. Sheryl looks at me in shock and whispers, 'how on earth are we going to fit these models, we have never seen before with fifteen looks in only twenty minutes? This is madness!' The designer next to me nudges my arm and points to Faye, as if to say is she for real?

'Christina!' Faye calls out again. 'Yes?' I reply. I almost feel like I was back at school and in danger of detention. Next, she utters the words that nearly make me pass out on those beautiful blonde wood floors.

'Christina, you are walking first, go fit your models, your twenty minutes start now!' Noooo, no, not me, why me, why me?

'Sherrrrryl,' I say like a loud speaker.

OK. Get a grip I tell myself. This is one of your 'put your big girl panties on' moments. Choose wisely Faye had said. Seriously…like who has time to choose wisely? I snap into action and say to Sheryl, 'I am going to apologize from now for the next several hours. If I yell at you or don't say thank when I should, I don't mean to. In saying that… quick, grab a look off the rack and start trying it on the models. Whoever fits it gets it, and make sure you get her name and her shoe size! Go!' Lady runs off.

Looking back I don't even know if we actually walked anywhere in the building that day. We just ran. Come to think of it we started running back in Sydney, and we pretty much hadn't stopped.

I start fitting the models, it was so frantic and stressful, and all my work had come down to this moment. I had to find the right model to wear the right outfit, it needed to look perfect and exactly as I had imagined it. Wishful thinking. There was no time, as before I knew it Faye was beside me and said, 'how many more have you got to fit?'

I rapidly counted and said, 'Oh no, I am only about half way through!' This was an almost impossible task I was thinking to myself. The models were so lovely and accommodating and could obviously sense my stress levels and rising panic. There were a couple of standout models, a lovely one called Sarah, she was such a honey, going out of her way to help me. There was one model called Gabriella, she had a gorgeous figure and each time we had fitted something on her it fitted like a glove. She had a Lilika body. I thought fast on the spot. OK, I will get Gabriella to do a few walks for me and then I won't have as many left to fit. Right, will that

Backstage at the show with my collection.

work? No time to process it. All this was running through my mind as Faye was standing there looking at me. Waiting for me to answer. I turn to Faye and ask for another five minutes. She briskly nods her head and walks off. I yell out to Sheryl, 'You do three more, and I do three, then we will be done!' Poor lady, she looked completely harassed, she had clothes hanging off her shoulders, pen behind her ear, shoes in one hand, helping a model into a dress with the other. WELCOME TO THE INDUSTRY I said to myself.

Faye calls out, 'Ok models, on to the next designer!' Our time was up. Really? Like seriously that was five minutes? Sheryl and I sit on our cases thinking what on earth just happened? I saw other designers looking at us like we had just landed from another planet. Right now though, I really don't care what they thought.

We still had not eaten or drunk a thing. I was busting for the bathroom and said to Sheryl, 'I'm just going quickly out front.'

She said, 'Ok, I am going to try and find us some coffee.' Oh, wonderful coffee.

Remember, we had not slept the night of our flight as we flew out of NZ in the evening, we had been working all that day then stepped into a twenty-seven hour flight. With all the stress that had entailed, no sleep on any of the flights. Then had arrived after our long haul flight, took an hour drive to our hotel. Had worked through the night snatching three hours sleep, we were doing ok! It was amazing we were still standing. For now we were, don't have much faith for later on in the day.

I run out through the backstage doors to the front, within seconds a lady comes up to me with a recorder saying, 'Christina?'

Christina Kilmister

Ahhhh. 'Yes?'

'I would love to interview you… can you please spare me some time now?' Wow… OK. I think well I am busting right now but there is no way I am passing up on an interview. 'Of course, I would love to!'

Now, this is what I absolutely love. Talking to people about my brand that I love so passionately. This is what all the hard work is for and I am going to enjoy it!'

After I had answered a ton of questions, thanked her and said my goodbyes, I headed for the bathroom. Sheryl would be wondering where I had got to.

At that exact moment she comes running through the doors saying, 'Quick, a photographer has been looking for you. He wants to do a photo shoot with one of your looks down on the street. Get a model and an outfit now and go.'

They did say New York was fast paced but this was getting ridiculous. Just then someone tugs on my arm.

'Excuse me-Christina? I am from Fashion TV and would love to interview you. I have been following you online and have been so looking forward to meeting you.' Another, ummm… okaaaaay.

I say to her, 'Oh, thank you so much! I am just heading downstairs to do a photo shoot, can I meet with you after that?" 'Wonderful, thank you,' she says.

As I am racing backstage to grab a model and outfit, still having not made it to the bathroom. Faye comes up to me, 'You are on in forty-five minutes, make sure you are ready'.

Where has the time gone? That seems to be all the words I have uttered since we arrived in the city.

I see Sheryl, go over to her and point out the fashion TV lady asking her to please go and tell her I will have to catch up with her a little later. The show is starting very soon. Lady runs one way, I run the other. Again, all we do is run.

When am I going to have two minutes to get to the bathroom, and possibly gulp down a coffee, let alone a bite of food? None girl, none. I must say I was loving it all the same. I had no idea I would have the interview interest so soon, and how cool to be doing a photo shoot with my model on the streets of Manhattan. I was determined to enjoy every moment of this madness.

What was amusing was the first lady that interviewed me started the interview with a cheeky smile saying, 'Oh, you are looking just a little bit posh.' It was great to see and hear the posh was cottoning on.

We did the shoot, which was awesome. I was heading back into the lift when another photographer asked if after the show she could get some shots of me and my models. Yes, I said, of course, and up I go into the lift to the top floor, where the show is. At this point I am starting to feel like I need a diary to schedule everything in.

I walked through backstage and saw Sheryl starting to line up the looks, ready to go. The models had all gathered around ready to be dressed, starting to bombard her with a hundred questions. I grabbed my moment and ran through the doors to the front, keeping my head down and making a beeline straight into the bathroom… I could not hang on any longer- finally.

I get backstage and Sheryl is talking to Faye looking perplexed. Faye turns to me and says, 'How many walks is Gabriella doing for you? Too many from what I can see on this list! She will be already walking when you have her down as wearing another look, you need to change your order right now! You have five minutes before your first model goes out!'

Here we go again.

Change the order? No way, it is all set with the models. I can't just completely redo the order in five minutes. All our carefully laid out looks with the matching accessories, with the model's names, shoes, were all in order. Where are the models? They were there before. I start calling their names, then in a moment they are all in front of me, asking me, 'so if I'm not wearing that dress, what accessories go with the other look?'

'But I can't be out fifth because the model before me is wearing...'

'So what number am I now?'

'The shoes I need with my look are now being worn by another model so what ones do I wear?'

WHERE is a tunnel? 'Cause I want one right now to crawl into and hide. I would have to confess those five minutes before the runway show started, would have to be up there with one of the most stressful times I have ever experienced. My music had started, I could hear it coming through the doors. Then I see my first model go out… eeeeeek, this is actually happening and now! Sheryl was meant to be in the front row with the video, but there was no way I could do backstage by myself so she had to stay with me. Poor lady, she was gutted as she was so looking forward to seeing the show.

Shot with one of my models outside the show.

The order couldn't have been completely sorted in our five minutes we had, duh… of course not! We had run out of time. We were just going to have to wing it. Sheryl and I were both ready by the door to grab the models as they came out, and get them into their next outfits.

Normally each model would wear one look, but oh no, not me, the order and models at this stage were completely up the pole. A pole that was tall and very bendy. We were literally throwing shoes and clothes across the room to dress and undress the models, so fast that it was literally a blur. Some had the wrong looks on but we didn't have time to get them out of them. And they had also got confused with what they were meant to be wearing.

I caught a few looks from the other designers backstage watching, a couple of them were snickering, and I heard one say, 'like seriously, has she got no order?!'

I felt like turning to her and screaming in her face, 'No I don't have any flipping order, do you have a problem with that?' But I just kept saying to myself 'come on girl, you can do this, you were just telling yourself before how much you love manic and excitement. Well, here it is. So deal with it.'

Sheryl was yelling out to me, 'What goes with this? Where is the model for this look? Who is wearing these shoes?' As some of the order that had been changed, I hadn't yet had the chance to tell her. So if you thought I would have been muddled, she was on another whole level altogether. She had no clue what was going on. I thought to myself, oh dear, I hope I don't give her a heart attack from this experience.

Gabriella, my ever so helpful model was my rock. She had still ended up doing a few looks, but was calm and helping me as much as she could, when she wasn't walking that was. She was amazing. I would definitely love to work with her again one day.

Every now and then Faye would yell at me, 'Where is your next model, she should be here at the door ready to walk, where is she?'

My stress levels were out of this world, but it was the loud clapping and cheers in the background, as the models were going out that gave me goose bumps in those moments. I was doing it, after all this time I was doing what I loved. Then all of a sudden a huge noise as the last model walks out.

Gabriella comes running back and says, 'it's our finale walk, come on!' I don't have time to check a thing I just step out onto the runway, thoroughly enjoying every moment of that walk. Gabriella grabbed my hand part way down the runway and squeezed it. I felt so proud of myself, of my designs, my models, lady, and just seeing my clothes on the international runway. Mostly though, that I had actually survived my first fashion show and in NYC. It was a moment I will never forget.

I met Sheryl backstage and she was just sitting on a chair, shoes off and looking completely exhausted. I gave her a big hug and thanked her so much for all her hard work and support.

She says, 'That was like a tornado… Is it always like this?' I don't answer. 'I mean, is it? I may not make five more years alive in the industry if this is what every show is like'. I smile to myself knowing that the worst is over, we will learn and we will get the hang of it.

I was almost too embarrassed to look at the other designers after the circus we had displayed backstage. I watched each designer calmly and quietly get each of their models ready, they were all lined up in order ready to go, they went out, they came back, it was impeccably done. More importantly, it was relevantly silent too.

Finale walk with the lovely Gabriella.

I felt disappointed for a moment, of the fiasco and disorganization of my show. You know what though… those designers do this all the time. I had no idea that I would only have twenty minutes to fit fifteen looks, on models I have never laid eyes on in my life. That I'd be first out on the runway to open the show, and have to change the whole order and models in five minutes before the show. I didn't know that we would also lose a whole day before the show to get organized. I didn't know any of that. So who cares if we were throwing clothes and shoes backstage (although I must confess, I did nearly hit another designer on the side of the head with a shoe, it was a gorgeous stiletto though). I created a collection in six weeks from absolutely nothing. A one off collection, did a photo shoot, produced an amazing press kit to take with me, (which a lot of others didn't have). So I will be proud! My big girl panties flipping rocked it!

We pack everything into our cases backstage and then head out to the front of the show. Sheryl found some food, at last. I took a bite of food and then the Fashion TV lady ran up to me.

'Can I please get that interview now? I have everything setup ready to roll'. She had waited all this time, I had actually forgotten. I walk over and sit down on the couch and have a great interview with her. She said, 'I would love to work with you again, so I will keep in touch.' After a hug and a selfie she goes.

I turn and walk straight into another lady who tells me she is from a NYC fashion magazine. 'I came here to look for talent and you were a complete standout. I loved your collection… it was amazing, and I want to feature you in our magazine. You are the only one here at this show I have offered a feature too. Well done, we will talk soon.' She says goodbye after handing me her card. Holey Moley… Ahhh what just happened? Woohoo… I was a little shocked and super happy all at once. I find Lady and tell her, who explodes with excitement, she had been busy networking herself.

After another photo shoot and two more interviews, along with numerous people from the public coming up to me telling me I was their favorite designer and they just loved the collection. Some of the ladies gave their details and wanted me to put some aside for them to buy. How good is that? It had been such an overwhelming, rewarding and fabulous day.

While Sheryl and I grabbed a rare moment to quickly go over some stuff – one of the ladies at the show, had told us to look up for a photo. So grateful that she had, as it had been so manic, there had been no opportunity to get one together.

We stayed a while longer to chat to everyone else and watch the rest of the show then went down to the street to get a taxi. We couldn't seem to get one to stop. We walked down a little further. Tried another spot. Then all of a sudden a taxi pulls next to us. We jump in quickly. The guy says to us, 'I can tell you have never been here before, when you

Sheryl and I.

hail a taxi you have gotta jump out and wave like you are going mad or we won't stop. You were standing there gently with your hand out on the pavement. You looked very pretty, but it's not the way to catch a ride'. Hmmm good to know. I think he thought it was pretty amusing.

We got back and ordered delicious room service again, as by this stage it was after 10 pm when we got in. We relaxed and caught up on the whole day, now laughing at all the nightmare moments and how we survived it. It was an amazing feeling to know it was over, and we had got such awesome feedback of our Kiwi brand. It had been a huge success. Happy dance. Make that a Zorba.

I turned on the laptop and emailed home, wishing Bevan was here too, he is so incredibly supportive and not being able to speak to him was driving me nuts. I would use Sheryl's phone tomorrow and call him. No matter what I did with my phone I just couldn't connect.

I felt so shattered but my mind was in overdrive, with what had happened in the last forty-eight hours. I was so looking forward to doing absolutely nothing tomorrow. We had three more days before we flew back home. I wanted to just be a tourist. Sheryl was out already, fast asleep. Thank goodness, no needle and thread in her hands tonight. I could not have done that show without her, she had been unbelievable.

Next thing I know, I hear those beeps again. Oh no, oh it's ok, the show is over! I look at my phone, it was three in the afternoon. I could not believe we had slept almost a whole day, but I guess it understandable after our recent adventures.

Sheryl wakes up, feeling great. I was happy as I was starting to worry after yesterday that I was going to kill her with stress. We were both starving, so we get dressed, layering up and hit the streets to find somewhere to eat. Stepping out onto the pavement, the air was crisp and the streets were hustling. People walking like they were on a mission, sneakers and backpacks on. Gee, how I loved this place.

We found a gorgeous little Thai restaurant, thinking we will just have a super early dinner and something light later on (yeah right I'm Greek remember, we don't do light). We had a wonderful time just chilling out and enjoying the atmosphere.

After that we just kept walking the grid, getting our bearings on where we were, and doing a little shopping. Once back at the hotel, before heading to our room, we, of course, have a wee detour past the gift shop for Lady! The guy in there loved our accent and kept telling us to say different words. Then he would just crack up laughing.

After saying 'fish and chips' several times, as that apparently was the funniest, I was starting to feel like a performing clown. I don't know how long we were in there, I had lost track. Before hopping in the lift, we made plans at the front desk to book our tours for the rest of the trip. Up in our room, I was keen to jump on the laptop and check my emails. New Zealand was 18 hours ahead of us. My daughter was keeping in contact with me all the time and updating Bevan. With the time difference and him working, it was a little tricky trying to get the right time to talk.

After replying to emails from Mum and Dad and the kids, I scroll down and see some new emails. I click the first one open. There were some fabulous photos that we had been sent through from the show. Also more emails from several other photographers with some teasers. There was still more to open. I click on the next one, start reading, and say to Sheryl, 'Ahhh lady?'

'What is it girl?!'

'There is an email here from a NYC fashion magazine saying they had sent one of their journalists along to the show. The report had come back that my collection was amazing, and they want to do a double page feature on Lilika! They have asked me when am I free do a photo shoot, and how long am I in town for?'

Sheryl, so excited shrieks so loud I almost skid off my chair with fright. OK, hang on. We will come back to that, there are more to open. Click – my eyes quickly scan the message. No way. A Boston TV show wants me to come and do an interview with them, when do I fly out? I read that one out to Sheryl too, her mouth just stays hanging open. And another one… click… what is going on?! I mean the show was only yesterday.

'They must have really liked the pink and blue huh?'

Another one… I read out loud, 'We would like to invite you to take part in Fashion Week for next season'. This time Lady's mouth just stays open, like a fly trap. Okaaaaaay, so where do I even begin. I need a coffee and a wine. In that order. Of course along with a side of fries, and fast.

We sit in disbelief with all the news – it is more than I had expected! To think I was unsure of the colors and the designs when I first turned up, knowing at the same time though in the back of my mind they would either love it or hate it. It was definitely different for there

BUT it was totally me, I was true to myself and to the brand, determined to not be led into the "norm". I was so proud of myself in that moment for just having faith and following through. It was worth it all, worth the stress, worth the manic work load, just worth it. Woopity woop woop!

We had a fabulous next three days. We were proper tourists. Everywhere we went, we were looking up at the beautiful buildings, a true sign you were a tourist. The architecture was stunning, Bevan would have loved it. You just couldn't help it. We found a super cute little place for breakfasts that we fell in love with.

We did the hop on, hop off bus tours, which on one day had us chasing the stops and doing a double loop just to find a shop that Lady was dying to visit. We got there eventually and she was one happy shopper. We went to the markets on another day, with a taxi driver who clearly wished he was in the Grand Prix, not knowing if we were going to make it dead or alive. We just hung on, cracking up as we were swung from side to side in the back seat, feeling slightly nauseous when we hopped out. But we still spent all morning shopping. We had a divine lunch at a little Italian restaurant, where the owner was trying to marry me off to his son who was serving us. After finding out I was part Greek, he told me many of his friends were Greek. He started saying a few words, so I mustered up a bit of Greek, which he just loved. We had desert on the house.

Over the short week we were there, we had beautiful dinners out along with amazing roof top dining in our hotel. Middle of the night walks through Times Square and shopping for gifts to take home. We did the Empire State of course and the Statue of Liberty. We did the works. Cramming it all in, and had an absolute ball. Lots of laughs, lots of shopping and a truckload of photos. We had met some wonderful people, and some amazing industry contacts for the future. Then the next thing we knew, the day arrived for us to head back to Kiwi-land.

I had been in contact with everyone that had emailed me with invitations etc. We were unable to make the photo shoots happen with our timing. Nor the Boston visit. We did have some awesome photos from the show though, so they would use those instead. I knew I would be back at some stage. Before we even left the US, I had been invited to two different Fashion Weeks. I knew there were exciting times ahead for my "posh little monster" as I had now nicknamed my brand, as she certainly was growing rapidly and undoubtedly very posh indeed.

What a ride it had been! After some fun pics with the very stylie concierge outside the hotel, we hop into our taxi and say goodbye to this amazing city.

Meeting the famous bull.

Mickey and co.

Time to be tourists on the bus.

Empire State.

Times Square night time selfie.

Photo with our cool concierge.

Thank you New York City, I am officially in love with everything about you. Till we meet again. We had a smooth ride home even if it was a long haul. We had no hassle stopovers, lots of yummy food and for Lady many more hot chocolates. We touched down on Kiwi soil, happy to be home. The guys were waiting for us in arrivals I throw my arms around Bevan, falling in love with him all over again, just at the sight of his handsome face. How I'd missed him! After a brief catch up, it was time to go our separate ways. Lady lives a couple of hours drive, south from Auckland, where we live.

I give Lady a huge hug and thank her for being a part of such a special and mad journey. One we won't forget in a hurry. We are both looking forward to a big sleep in our own beds, that's for sure. I grab Bevan's hand and chatting non-stop walk to the car, hop in, and we head for home. Silently thankful for my amazing experience, what a learning curve it had been. I have taken away so much from it. I have learnt even more about myself and also about myself as a designer. The word resilience coming to my mind once again. I am not the type of person to just buckle in and give up. No way, it is not who I am.

As I have mentioned before there will always be naysayers in your life. That is a prime example of when you have to be resilient and persistant, dig those fabulous stilettos in and stand your ground, listening to what your heart is telling you. They will try to bring you down, to plant a seed of doubt, to make you second guess yourself. Well now, I just say, bring them on, as all they do is make me want to push even harder and be even better. It's actually brilliant as all it does is make you even stronger. The highs and the lows made my journey what it was. Without the lows, I wouldn't have learnt, and without the highs I wouldn't have appreciated. I definitely felt like I had achieved all of those.

I cannot wait to see what is next for myself and my beautiful posh little monster. Bring it on!

Don't talk to me if you want cookie cutter clothes. I don't do ordinary, I do big pops of color, with a dash of bling and a dollop of posh.

Maybe I shouldn't have called her a "posh little monster", as that's just what she has become. Beautifully dressed of course, and oozing class, but a little monster all the same. Me, I haven't stopped running, well not literally. Running in another sense of the word. One thing after the other has happened since returning from NYC, it has been wonderful but slightly chaotic. One could just call it madness… just how I love it. I feel totally and abundantly blessed and happy with my life. I get to wake up and do what I love every day. I am hands on with the business, having my fingers in many pies (plum and apple with a scoop of cream of course). I believe in being as personal as I can with my business, she is my baby and I know exactly how I wish her to be. I try to directly deal with as many people as I can, as I think it's important to have that connection. I want to be the face of the business.

Only I have the passion and love for it. The hours I put in don't matter, nor does the time of day. I can't imagine anyone else saying or doing the same thing. It is like when you are a new mum and you have that perfect little human in your arms. Yes, they may keep you awake all night, they may take every ounce of energy that you have BUT without a doubt, you show up, you get up and you give that baby all the love in the world no matter what the time of day. Get it? Yes, I understand it's not a new born baby but the similarity in what you will do when you love and are committed to something. Plus, I could possibly be a tad of a perfectionist (although a friendly one) and a wee control freak. That's all good, I am happy to admit that as being hands on with Lilika has made it what it is today. I wouldn't have it any other way. I want a boutique brand, I want a personal brand, I want people to know that it is my brand and I work my brand.

Hmmm…now…where do I begin? I have a lot to fill you in on. You know the drill. You should be parked up already on that comfy sofa, with your feet up, hot chocolate, tea or a wine in hand. Silky pjs on and ready to hear all about my latest journey.

After I arrived back from Manhattan, I caught up on some much needed sleep, in my own bed. The bliss of it. I felt like after all that excitement I would have slept for a year. There was a huge load of unpacking to do and sorting of the collection and accessories. There was just SO many shoes but one must always have options in fashion. These are things that bring the whole look together. As I was pulling the different looks out, already the memories of it all came flooding back. From the moments of feeling completely out of my depth and overwhelmed, to the moments of pure pride seeing those girls walk out in my creations. I learnt so much from that experience, as a designer, a business owner and just a woman following her heart and living her passion. When you literally throw yourself out there into the world, your heart hanging off your sleeve for all to see, whether it be a perfectly shaped heart or whether it be a heart that is a little rough around the edges – you are showing the world yourself. It will either make you or break you. It made me. It taught me even more, that fear and that uncomfortable feeling of being outside that "box" that makes you squirm, and ask, what on earth am I doing. THAT beautiful people, is the best feeling you can have. I have learnt that if it isn't just a little bit daunting, a little bit scarey, and at the same time excites, it just isn't 'big' enough. So if you get that, grab it with both hands and don't let go, make it happen!

Back to where I was… I was starting to relax, for a moment. After the NYC show, as you may remember, I was already being contacted with multiple invitations to show, before I even got on the plane to come home to Kiwiland. It didn't stop there. The following two weeks once I got home, was verging on the ridiculous, almost every day I got invitations from around the US to show my creations, including Paris and London.

I was also contacted by Hearst in the UK to feature in Cosmopolitan, with them stating that they feel Lilika would be a perfect fit for their magazine. It was really deliciously amazing but a bit overwhelming. I relished every moment. Bevan would come home most nights and I would tell him someone new had contacted me. To the point, he would just walk in the door and say, 'So who today?'

We ended up with twelve invitations to show in that time. Not counting the ones while I was in NY. Our double page feature was soon to be published in the NYC glossy fashion magazine. This was from the contact that had come to the show and approached me afterward. My gorgoeus French country coffee table was now going to become even more fabulous.

The moment I got back I was already late for the next NZ collection, as the invite to go to Manhattan had put everything else behind. So, yet again I hit the ground running to get onto the collection, photo shoot and then produce it. As we are a season ahead in NZ, everything is out extra early compared to the rest of the world. I decided to roll out a mini collection to be able to make things work. Then of course it was just catch up from then on. It felt, for a little while though, like we were always on the back foot, chasing the seasons. I kept reminding myself that we would get there and it is what it is. I mean it was well worth going to NY as look what we got out of it for Lilika.

It was then time, in amongst all that was going on, to decide if we would take up one of the invitations and if so, which one?

There was not a doubt in my mind that we had to be back on the runway again. I had got the bug, the beautiful exhilarating bug that only another designer understands. The huge high after the massive push to make it happen. Hearing your music go on and then boom… it's all go! I wanted that again, I wanted it all.

So we decided after some deliberation that we would head to LA to show and also combine a holiday at the end of the business. I had family in San Diego I had never met but always wanted to. I had kept in contact with my cousin Donna who last saw me when I was one year old when she was babysitting me, with my eldest sister Rachel. As soon as we started contact online, there was a connection between us that was instant. Like we had known each other all our lives. We were kindred spirits. We felt more like sisters than cousins. So the plan would be to stay with her and hubby Jose after the show. My Auntie (Dad's twin sister) Jos'e was going to come over from Vancouver to see us. Wow, so much was going on and Lilika was making it all happen. This time Lady would sit it out and Bevan would come with me.

So all the planning began. I had more notice than last time but still not that much in the big picture of things. It was going to be close to make the new collection. I feel though, after the tiny amount of time I had to design and produce for NYC, I could do anything. It had given me the confidence. Not going to another show was just not an option for me, I almost work best under pressure, (although some family members may not agree with that haha). Oh yay, it was play time all over again. How I just adored choosing the fabrics for my designs. Then the icing on the cake is shopping for all the accessories to complete the final look. All so exciting. I was in my manic glorious element.

I did a variation on a couple of the designs, as I had such awesome feedback on the NYC collection, the people from the show thought that it would do really well there. Initially, they thought I would be showing that same collection. Oh no, me being me, I decided I wanted to do a whole new one didn't I? (Eye roll).

Of course it wasn't just designing and making the new collection, it was also having to do a new photo shoot for it, as we needed "look books" and campaign photos to send through and take with us.

My lovely friend Nikki, who is also a hair and make up artist said she would love to be part of this new adventure. She was also based in Auckland where I live. Nikki did gorgeous hair and makeup for the shoot and we had lots of fun. Sheryl would sit this one out, she was still getting over NYC!

At least when I returned from LA, the collection would only be a little bit late going out for NZ. That would be great.

I thoroughly enjoyed myself, the collection came out beautifully, I was so happy with it. I went a little mad with the buttons but that is my thing. Our trademark. Lilika is all about the extra, finer, finishing details on the designs. My mother once again sewed every button on, to every sample. I think she was ready to sign herself up to a spa retreat out in the middle of nowhere for three months after it was all done. Once again we were working together, every garment that was designed and made was under the brand name, her name.

That in itself was special. We would talk often of Manoula how much she would have loved what we were doing. My mother has such an eye for creation, she is always so excited when a new design is completed. She would say, 'oh, I can just picture this walking down the runway!' Most times she would come accessory shopping with me; she loved putting together all the looks as much as I did. Talk about being another version of her ... peas in a pod.

Lots of the time we were in fits of giggles, some I think just from tiredness and the big deadline to finish it all in time. A silly tiredness. Others, just because we laugh a lot together. Bevan always says to everyone when it's over, 'oh I have my wife back again!' He pretty much just leaves me to it during this phase. He knows I am there but not there. When he talks to me, I am listening but it's really not sinking in. I am completely living and breathing the collection. He is the most amazing support and just gets how I work and what I need to do. That I will go until I'm done and done to perfection. I am in my own little world of color and creativity... like a bear in hibernation. I do venture out to eat and drink though. I love food too much.

Mother and I.

Time was nearing, the look book was now all completed and it was time to ship off the collection to the US.

Oh my, the feeling of letting my babies go in a box on a plane, with the absolute hope of seeing them again when we arrived ourselves, was torture. My fingers and toes were crossed. I would not sleep well until I knew they had landed safe and sound in Hollywood. A week later I get the fabulous news they had arrived. Hip hip hooray, now I just had to get myself there. Oh and husband too of course.

I had designed the dress I was to wear to the finale show, something different to the other designs but still cohesive within the collection. After the praise for my last outfit in NYC I knew I had to do it again and I always will. Why wouldn't I take the amazing opportunity to wear my brand? There is nothing else I would ever want to wear. It would be bright and playful and there would be gold, oh how I love my gold. You will know that already by now. It would have lace too, as I love the pretty and feminine feel of lace paired with a strong design.

Sending off my precious cargo.

I had booked in to get my eyelashes done as I thought they are great to have when going away. All I needed was a touch of bronzer and a swipe of gloss and I would be good to go. I love to keep it light and fresh when traveling. Also, I thought with the shows and different events on, it would be a busy schedule. I would be already half done, having a fabulous set of lashes. So I got those done the day before we were to fly out. They looked amazing. But I had strict instructions for them not to get wet, no rubbing etc... so I was aware of getting them through that first initial stage so nothing happened to them.

We were all packed up and on our way to the airport on the other side of the city. Once again I was amazed how it had all come together and we had made it happen. I must admit after the NYC show and others at home it had given me a lot more confidence, so this time at least I knew to a degree what to expect, and how things would run. That was a way better feeling than literally walking into the dark, arms out in front of me, having no clue what was going on.

We arrived at the airport and checked in and chilled out until our flight was called. We had a stopover in Honolulu and then would go on to LA from there. My NY flight was twenty-seven hours in total, this was a little less, so I was happy about that. Those twenty-seven hours had felt like an eternity, especially when I had been unwell as I was.

It was still a very long flight though. New Zealand is so far away from the rest of the world. Everything was on schedule and we reached Hawaii on time. I loved that blast of hot air that hits you when you step out through the airport doors. We love going on holidays in the islands and make sure we get away every year, it is that same feeling when you get off the plane and walk across the tarmac.

We had the sunshine for a very short time then caught our connecting flight. Before we knew it we had landed in LA. Wow, what a smooth, stress free trip compared to last time. It was midnight when we landed so by the time we got into our hotel it was the early hours of the morning we were shattered. All I wanted was a hot shower and bed. So I hop into the shower, it was divine, my back had been feeling a bit sore after all that sitting so having the hot water beating on it felt amazing. I get my cleanser and start washing my face and neck. The shower felt so good after that flight. Wait... what's that on my face? It's feeling all gritty, my face, neck and my hands. I had some candles on in the bathroom, so it was a dimmed flickering light. I turn off the shower and take a look at my hands, completely confused as to what this stuff was. Then to my utter horror, it dawns on me. I see all these black things. OH MY GOODNESS MY LASHES! I had forgotten all about my beautiful new lashes and had just gone ahead and scrubbed my face, along with my lashes, right off my eyes. I was gutted. I had been so tired, I wasn't thinking about anything else but just getting under that glorious hot water. There were so many little black things everywhere, stuck on me, in the bottom of the shower. They looked like little creepy crawlies. Well there wasn't much hope in having anything left on my eyes. I turned the shower back on and rinsed myself off, wrap the lovely thick soft towel around me and stepped out. I really didn't want to look in the mirror. But I did. OH. It really was awful. They were all pretty much gone apart from the odd ones here and there. I looked like a spider with growth problems. There were lots of stubbies and then some tallies. I couldn't believe this had happened. Yet in saying that, I certainly seemed to attract situations.

Bevan calls out, 'Are you ok in there Baby? I keep hearing these sighs and oh no's!'

I walk in and say, 'Ahh yeah, well I kind of just washed my whole set of lashes off didn't I?' He looks at me a little bit blank, and I can see he is trying to hide a smile, but can also see how upset I am.

'Well babe there are still some left…isn't there?'

YEAH NUH. There ain't enough of those puppies to look like anything even near fabulous. It looked like a rat had been at my eyes. Oh well, I desperately needed sleep and there was nothing I could do about it. What's done is done. I sink into the bed and the beautiful silky sheets. You idiot! I tell myself and promptly fall asleep.

Next thing I know light is shining through the room and it looks like a beautiful clear blue day. Yay, we are here. Then, I remembered my rat's eyes, oh no…. We had two days before the show but those two days would be doing fittings and be pretty busy.

The first day we were jet lagged, so we were pleased we could relax for the first day. We had a hotel close to the action, the show was right in downtown LA.

The next night we had a designer's dinner, where we met everyone and networked with some industry players that had been invited. I met a young guy who was sitting opposite me who was also a designer. We got chatting, and he reminded me so much of my son and was the same age. We had a great night and I had the chance to wear one of my designs. I always LOVE dressing up. I had ended up making a few different ones so had something to wear for every day during that week. I wore a high low frock with gold and white and it was a huge hit. We were having a ball.

Bevan looked handsome as per usual, and we always have so much fun together. He is my mate in life. I was so happy to have him by my side. He had really become a part of the business but he was still a little out of his comfort zone. He was a chippie by trade

Selfie with Bevan, heading out for a walk to explore.

With my gorgeous hubby at the Designers dinner.

(a builder), and he grew up in the beautiful beach town of Mount Mangaunui. About three hour's drive from where we currently live. He grew up pretty much with a hammer in one hand and a surfboard in the other. The Mount is where I met him one New Year's eve when I was there on a weekend away from Auckland where I grew up. Anyway, I digress, that is another story altogether!

Back to where I was. So, of course, he had never had anything to do with fashion in the past. Yet here he was in LA in amongst it and up to his eyeballs. He was amazing and was learning more and more about the industry and how it all worked. He is a really cruisy guy. We balance each other to perfection. I would run around at a million miles an hour and he would just be saying, 'it's ok baby, don't worry, it will all come together.' He was without a doubt my rock. My gorgeous, gentle, kind rock that I couldn't imagine life without. Hey, but of course that's why I married him. To share this experience with him was very cool indeed.

The next morning it was another clear blue beautiful day, even though it was their autumn, to us it was still warm and summer-like. We walked everywhere; if it was not too far away we walked. We did notice though that not many people actually walked. We had some surprised looks from people at the show when we told them we walked. We could have got a taxi but we loved walking back home, and on such gorgeous days, why wouldn't you want to? Everything we needed was already at the show so all I had was my handbag and iPad to carry. When we did catch a taxi to the first show and party, we told the driver we had a wander all around the city. He told us we shouldn't have done that. It wasn't a good idea to walk. Oh well. We are Kiwis, it's all good.

Since my accident when I had to give up riding Atlas, I had taken up walking instead as you know. It was important for me to keep my back strong and also for me to get out into the fresh air. So I walked early every morning for an hour along the beach, which is just down the hill from where we live. I guess what I'm trying to say is that walking is just what we do.

It was time to go. I put on my gorgeous flowy chiffon high low top. It was white with pops of beautiful tiny flowers on it in bright pinks and yellow. One of the frocks from the collection was made out of the same. It was a sleeveless top and dropped down in a big scoop at the back. I had paired it with my three quarter fitted white jeans with diamanté buttons and cuffed them up at the bottom to a three quarter length. My favorite Steve Madden wedges that were nude with a hot pink fluro ankle strap completed the look. I was trying hard not to focus on my eyes too much, I just put mascara on them to try to even and fill out the gaps. There was an awful lot of gaps, and the ones that were still on were pretty tight so I couldn't get them off and looked super long compared to the others. Let's just put it down to a right royal screw up. Moving on!

We head off to the location as it was the first fitting day. I had already been sent through shots of different models in the collection, along with all their details. A lot of the casting had been done but I needed to actually see the models in the designs and decide for myself. I also wanted to make sure I booked the models I wanted. This time around I didn't want any stress and wanted it to be as organized as possible.

While I went backstage to meet the models and the rest of the gang, Bevan stayed out the front. He was happy to just mooch around and see if there was anything he could do to help. He would even be happy to just park it up in the sun for a bit too.

I saw my rack in the corner, setup ready for me, the collection was hanging up. It was weird to see it there when the last time I saw it I was packaging it up into the box all the way back at home. Or should I say I was literally sitting on the box to make it all fit in. Looking at it, I was in love with the colors and the designs all over again. It was posh, playful and full of personality, I was so excited to actually see these on.

All my shoes and accessories were numbered for each look and laid out on the main table in the middle of the room, with some other stuff that wasn't mine at the other end. I remember thinking, wow, that isn't much stuff for all these designers. The designers must have all their own things at their racks. Looking around back stage, people were running back and forth all over the place, with models whipping in and out of clothes. Shoes going on, going off, it was all happening back here. I loved it.

Speaking of shoes though, the next moment I see someone go up and start looking through my sets of shoes and jewelry not quite sure what to make of it, was she admiring them? Picking her way through, then she looks at a pair, picked them up and started to walk away with them.

Ummm… hello! I went over and said to her, 'Hi, um, those are my shoes for my collection.' She said, 'Oh sorry, I thought they were for everyone!' I thought, oh dear this could prove to be a problem as I walked back to my corner. I just carried on working my way through my selected models trying the looks on. I had two assistants to help me backstage, they were great, especially one, Priscilla. She knew exactly what I needed and what to do. Totally on my wave length.

We had some fun together. I had someone else go up and grab another set of my stuff off the table and managed to catch her in time too. It was just so busy back there and we were all working to a time frame as the models had to go soon. One of the producers came back stage and introduced me to a gorgeous young lady called Emma whose dream was to walk in an LA fashion show. She loved Lilika and wanted to wear something from the collection. We chose her the perfect look to wear down the runway, a beautiful and very girly lace dress. She said she felt like a princess in it, so we knew it was definitely the one. She was a very special little lady. We got on well straight away and she had the loveliest, sweetest mum with her called Maria. I would see them both again tomorrow for the show but in the meantime I would carry on with all the fittings. The first show was on tonight and the models needed to move on to the designers that were showing, so they could get ready. As they were waiting for hair and makeup, or coming out from it, we would grab the chance and fit them for looks. My show was tomorrow night. The last lot of models would be coming in tomorrow for fittings. I had just over half of the collection fitted, the rest I would finish tomorrow. I'm sure that will be fine.

Selfie backstage with my lovely assistant Priscilla

I hadn't even had a chance to pop out front to see how Bevan was going, as it had been non stop back there. Looking at the time though, I had been gone for ages. I hang all my collection back on my rack in correct order and went out the front to look for him.

I walked down the other end to the space and see a group of people standing there, looking up watching something. I reach them and follow their eyes, then do a double take! Ahhh what? There is Bevan right at the top of the space on this super high scaffolding, standing there lifting the catwalk entrance wall into place with a couple of other guys. Well, to be fair he was the only one out on the end of this scaffolding, while the others were on a different lower part and covered from head to toe in safety gear. There is my Kiwi chippy walking up there like it's a footpath!

'Err, yeah, that's my hubby up there'.

They couldn't believe it. 'He should have safety gear on, what is a designers husband doing up there anyway?'

I was wondering the same thing myself. I was trying not to be too concerned about him way up there, I did know that he was an experienced and confident builder. He had been building since he was eighteen years old. The other thing is, back at home he is used to clambering up and over stuff as they don't get all geared up like they do here in the US. They pretty much just have their tool belts on and that's it, the majority of the time. He told me later that he didn't want to sit there doing nothing so went over and asked the guys if he could do anything to help out. Bless him, it was so like him, he ended up playing a big part of getting all the production side finished and ready for the show. Kiwis SO rock! Especially my super cute Kiwi.

I sat down for a while and relaxed after the hours of running around at the fittings. It was so lovely feeling the sun on me. We had just come out of a dreadful cold, wet winter in NZ. I was just relishing the heat. For most of that day, I had pulled clothes over heads then I took them off, I put feet into shoes and I pulled them off. One after the other, after the other. I shall be doing it in my sleep tonight for sure I thought.

Not long after I had been sitting down, a top fashion influencer that was there for the event, who was from Germany, came over to me, saying she loved the brand and would I be happy for her to wear something at the show tonight. Of course, how fabulous! So I went backstage. Her name was Sarah and she was such a darling and we had lots of fun together, trying different things on and then she saw my gold and white striped dress I had worn to the designer's dinner the night before. It was not actually part of the runway collection. Fitting her perfectly, she looked gorgeous, so off she goes to the front row to wait for the show to start.

The first show was starting soon and there was a buzz of excitement in the air. After chatting away for a bit and logging all the fitting details and info into my iPad, Bevan came over and said he was done. By this time the space was starting to fill up and we decided we would stay on and watch the show. I was excited to think this time tomorrow would be my turn. I glance down the other end and see that lovely lady who had come back stage.

Earlier on during fittings when we were all running around here, there and everywhere, one of the team had come through with a TV show lady called Gaby Natale. She was covering the show. She wanted to interview me, which was great, but right then I still had so many more models to fit and I had to grab them while they were still there. I said to her, 'I would love to speak with you but could I do it a little later, when I have the fittings done?'

She was fine with that. And there she was right now, I had forgotten completely about it. So I walk down the end to where she was with all the press and ask her if she is free now to do the interview. She was and ran through with me what we would do. Then all of a sudden there was a microphone in front of me and a camera in my face. The sun was quite bright so I felt like I was squinting terribly. I had left my sunglasses just behind me in my bag. I had been going like

a mad thing all day, any makeup I did have on would have come off by now. Oh well no time. Let us not even mention the eyelashes shall we. They were certainly no confidence booster!

Ok, off we go.

She asked me all sorts of things, from my inspiration for the collection, to what is my favorite thing to travel with. Gaby was such a sweetie and had a lovely bubbly personality. We got on so well, took a few selfies and said we would keep in touch. Update – we did, after I was back home we caught up again. She has worn Lilika to events since. I learnt after the show, she is actually president of her own media company *Agarna Media* and her own TV show *Superlatina*. Over that following year she made history in winning three Emmy's back to back, not to mention multiple nominations, along with becoming an Author. She is an amazing inspiration and her drive is to support and empower women with everything she does. We have become friends and I am super proud of her. She will be wearing lots more of Lilika.

Selfie with my gorgeous friend Gaby.

Back to where I was... Gaby would be back to see my show tomorrow.

As I was walking away from that interview, a guy comes up to me saying he was waiting for me to become free. He said he also wanted to interview me and was with some fashion magazine. So I happily answered all his questions about how I started in the industry and many more. He took some photos and said he would be coming back tomorrow for my show. After that I went back to my little posy in the sun that was rapidly now starting to set. Just lapping it up.

It would be so great to just sit back and enjoy the show. It was not too long after and we took our seats. It was an open space where all the seating was and the night sky was twinkling high above us, it looked amazing. Especially along with all the little lights on in the towering buildings surrounding us. It was so gorgeous, the air had cooled down to the point I was wishing I had another layer.

Then the music booms out of the speakers and the first model stomps her way down the runway. Yay, here we

Gaby wearing a Lilika piece to an event after the show.

go! I think it was the second or third designer out and I was looking at the outfits coming down. I noticed a cool chunky gold bangle on the models arm and then the following one had a bright pink one similar. Hang on! Those were mine! I glance down and there behold were my, one of a kind shoes on the models feet. I whack Bevan in the arm with my elbow, he looks at me.

'Umm what is wrong with you?'

More models go down and I see more of my shoes and accessories coming out. I was wound up at this point as these were things I had especially chosen from NZ, one of a kind, to go with my Runway looks. Chosen because I knew no one else would have them here. There they go right before my eyes, completing someone else's look. Uggg. Then I hear a lady behind me say,

'Wow… check out the shoes in this group, I haven't seen anything like them here'. Well hello lady, no you haven't because they are not from here, and they shouldn't be on anyone's feet right now. I didn't say it out loud of course but oh my I really did feel like it. I was really feeling like getting my freak on. In a Greek kind of way.

I decide to get up when there is a break in designers and walk backstage, as there was no way I was going to have any more of my stuff coming down the runway. Backstage was mayhem and as soon as I turned the corner I realized it was a silly idea to go. So I went over and said to the backstage manager not to let anyone else wear my things and hands off to that end of the table. Then I go back out the front and calmly take my seat. Bevan looks at me and pats my knee. We enjoyed the rest of the show.

We had just realized we hadn't eaten all afternoon or had dinner and we were ravenous. So we go out to the food truck and grab something to eat. Oh yes. You know what they had don't you… Fries. Fries, fries, fries with a big fat capital F. I asked for a huge scoop and a gourmet chicken burger. Delicious. Ahhh, I felt like I could function again. Maybe if I had a full stomach I could have handled the runway issue a little better.

After staying for a little after the show we headed back to the hotel as it was another big day tomorrow, well my big day and I wanted to get a decent sleep. We were both still feeling a little

Loved having this gorgeous man with me.

jaded with jetlag. Bevan had also been building for hours too. We did have an awesome night though.

We let ourselves into the room and collapsed with big sighs of contentment. It had been a good day and we had full bellies and were now about to hit the sack. Wonder if that is a Kiwi saying… we obviously do have a lot of Kiwi sayings, as have had many blank looks when we say some stuff. We get looked at like, what did you just say and what does that mean? Pretty much what planet do you come from? You may have already experienced that in this book. It is quite funny as I had no idea we had our own language.

After a fabulous sound sleep, we wake up the next morning and head straight out for breakfast. We already have a favorite place that has the best, freshest yummiest croissants. I am like a walking zombie until I have a sip of coffee, Bevan knows me well and doesn't try to have too deep a conversation until its coffee time. Yay, it's show day! Woop woop!

Today the goal is to get all my final looks fitted and locked in, make sure the garments have all been pressed to perfection and we had the running order down pat. The show is a little later in the evening. I had my friend coming in from outside LA to watch the show and I was so excited to see her again. It had been years when I first met her back home at a fashion show. I was still in my corporate job then. We were both walking in it for a charity show. We hit it off straight away and within a week we had met up and gone out together. She had a fabulous, larger than life personality. She was all about having fun and living life to the absolute fullest. Being a coach and presenter she just naturally connects and inspires those around her. She was also gorgeous with the most amazing figure and I couldn't wait to get her in Lilika. Sadly her time was up and she had to leave NZ along with her lovely young daughter Natalie, to go to London to work. So we didn't have long together before she left the country but we have kept in contact over the years. When I knew I was going to LA I couldn't wait to tell her. She would be coming to the show. Well actually, she was meeting us at our hotel and we would all go in together. After the models had been fitted the plan was to go home, relax for a bit and get ready for the show.

The fittings took a lot longer than I thought as all the models were turning up at different times so I had to wait for a few to arrive before I could fit them. After some time they were finally all chosen, fitted and noted along with photos taken of the complete looks. I was happy. The designs looked fab on the models and I couldn't wait to see them hit the runway.

There was no time for walking, we grabbed a taxi and left for the hotel, my friend Tami would be arriving soon. We had something to eat when we got back, had showers, and by then Tami arrived.

After squealing and kissing and hugging, talking non stop, we get dressed. I was taking my finale walk dress with me and wearing an Aline bright print mini dress until show time. It was super cute with a gorgeous cut and little pleated cap sleeves. I pop on my wedges and I am ready to roll. Everything else is already at the show, off we all go. Tami and I yabber away in the back seat taking selfies and starting to catch up on many years in the space of a taxi ride.

Bevan meanwhile, is talking NZ with our driver. The driver is cool and we message him now to book in a ride. We know he will turn up on time and get us where we need to go. He took us to the first designer's event and we used him ever since. He was a lovely guy and so reliable.

He drops us right outside the event. It looks amazing, everything is set up ready to go. We walk down the huge wide red carpet stairs and down to the runway space. There are gorgeous lantern type lights hanging all the way across and at night look awesome. I say goodbye to Tami and Bevan and head backstage, they just hang out in the front.

Reunited – my lovely friend Tami and I, on the way to the show.

Selfie with the adorable Emma.

I meet up with my assistant and double check that all the looks are in their correct order. Unfortunately, my favorite assistant Priscilla was not there for my show night. My special young lady Emma turns up with her mother Maria. She is so excited to be walking in the show. She sees straight away how busy I am and that there is a lot going on so gets in and helps me.

She was such a huge help, assisting me with some styling and last minute steaming, you could tell she just loved being in the environment. Fashion was her thing and was something she wanted to do in the future. We had some giggles along the way and had fun in amongst all the craziness. I was then just told by the backstage manager, Denise, a couple of the models hadn't turned up, so suddenly I had to try and find new models and refit them. Which also meant switching some shoes and accessories around as of course all the models had different sized feet, and the new models I was fitting were different to the ones I had already booked in to walk. The young guy I meet at the designer's dinner who reminded me of my son, came over and said he could help for a few minutes. So sweet of him, so he helped me fit a couple of models then went out front after that. He had his show last night and it was awesome.

Time was moving quickly and just as I was really starting to feel stressed I see Tami walk in to the back. Hallelujah!

'Perfect timing… I need some help, can you stay back here and help me, please? Not all the assistants had turned up yet so the one that was helping me had been called elsewhere.' So I finished with Tami's help fitting the new models. Right, so now I was back to where I was when I first turned up. Phew!

Tami was awesome and it was great to have her there backstage, although that had not been the plan. She was chatting away with all the hair and makeup girls, everyone always loves her wherever she is. As we are going through some things, Denise comes up to me and says that the order has now changed and I have now moved back a position. The models that were walking for me are now having to walk for the designer in front of me, in my old spot. Ummm… but how and why?! She walks away and I look at Tami. I have a feeling come over me that reminded me very much of NY. Oh no. Not again. Okaaaaay… so let me think, what exactly does this mean?

Tami says, 'it's ok sister. So what do we need to do? Don't worry I will stay back here until the show starts.'

Thank goodness for that, bless her beautiful heart. The assistants are running around everywhere, trying to catch one is like chasing a wild rabbit through an open field. Then if you do catch one they look at you like a possum at night with the headlights on them. Yeah, nuh… they were not going to be working for me tonight. If I didn't have Tami helping me I could have been in trouble. Sheesh! Seriously though, how do I attract these situations on a regular basis? Stupid question girl. Why do you always ask yourself this same question girl? I then remembered that Bevan would be wondering where on earth Tami was, as initially she had just come backstage to wish me luck for the show. So she dived out the front and told Bevan how manic things were back there and she was staying on to help out. He was happy chatting away to the guy sitting next to him.

Ok. So basically all the models I had carefully selected and fitted and organized in running order were now going to be coming straight off the runway from the designer in front of me. The big issue was, that when I needed to be hitting the runway, some of them wouldn't have time to get back there and get into my looks. As my collection would already be walking as they were coming off. OH MY. So I was told that I will just have to grab whatever free model was there at the time. Are you freaking kidding me?! But they haven't been fitted or anything, I don't even know if they can fit the clothes. Or what they will even look like in them. Then it dawned on me, that of course the selected shoes and accessories will now be completely turned upside down, as I don't know if the models will even fit the shoes. I can feel my temples start up. No, those little hammers are not coming here to LA.

Tami looked at me. 'This is seriously crazy back here, like wow this is madness!'

YIP hello! The show had just started, all I could do was completely wing it with the models, it is what it is, and there was nothing I could do about it. There was a designer beside me who was literally falling apart. I said to her, 'Look don't worry, tell me what needs doing and I'll help you'.

She looked at me almost in tears and said, 'This is my first show and I need help I'm up next and my models need dressing!' So I got straight into it and started dressing the models, she was on in a minute and the models were still coming in.

I was calling out to her, 'What model wears this look? Quick who wears these shoes?' Once again it was mayhem and not even my mayhem. I was literally shoving those clothes on the models, jamming shoes on feet, it was a total blur. Then the last one walks out and the designer comes and hugs me.

'Thank you so much! I will help you when you are on, I promise.'

That now wasn't far away. Tami goes back to the front to join Bevan, still in awe as to what was going on backstage. Apparently saying to him, he told me later, 'Oh that is some crazy stuff going on back there!' Sarah, the lovely fashion influencer that wore my dress to yesterday's show (I found out later was a TV reality show host and has her own media company, among other things) came up to me and said she would love to wear another Lilika look to tonight's show and to film an episode for her show. She ended up wearing two different looks over the evening, we did a little bit of filming together. One of the looks we put her on the catwalk as she looked so good.

After that, I went over to the table where all my stuff was and double checked all the line-up of shoes and

Sarah and I selfie.

accessories were in place and ready to go. Hang on! There are two pairs of shoes missing, no way. What was it with these people and my stuff? I look around and see a pair of shoes in an assistant's hand.

I go over and get them off her, telling her they are mine and do not touch or take anything on that part of the table. Ever so nicely of course. I put them back in place, now for the other pair, which was actually my finale shoes, so crucial I have them. I glance to the left and see them sitting nice and pert, pretty and glittery on the floor. Sitting in front of a designer's rack, clearly teamed up with an outfit. Hold me back!

I go over to her and say to the assistant, 'Why are my shoes sitting here?'

She replies, 'I didn't know they were yours, she,' (pointing at the designer) 'told me to get them'.

This designer had already taken a pair on the first day, so she knew full well they were my shoes. Meanwhile, the music was pumping and I was not far off now in order to go on. I went over to the designer and pick up the shoes.

'You have my shoes, why do you have them, you know they are mine'.

'No… they aren't yours, they are mine'.

I was stunned, ahh… what are you playing at girlfriend?

'These are not your shoes, I brought them from New Zealand for the show… These are not your shoes'. I could slowly feel my blood pressure creeping up. I need this like a hole in the head.

Next thing I know she snatched the shoes out of my hands and yells at me, 'I want these shoes they are perfect for my look, they are mine!

Since I have been back in the industry I feel like I have found myself rooted to the spot quite a few times and here I was again. I actually could not believe that this woman was picking a fight with me over my shoes and also right now when I was about to go on. I am so not a confrontational person and mostly accused of being too much of a softie. There are a few things though that really bring out the Greek in me. Don't mess with my kids, my horse, my husband… or my shoes. When she grabbed those off me, all I could think about was my finale walk, the model and having no shoes, not only no shoes but these were absolutely perfect for the look.

I grabbed the shoes and pulled them towards me saying quietly and trying hard to keep my cool. 'These are not your shoes, ask Denise as she knows these arrived in a box from NZ. They. Are. Mine.' I had a fleeting image of the movie Nemo with all the seagulls squawking mine, mine, mine! I felt like I was on repeat and also dealing with a five year old child. It was unbelievable.

She pulled the shoes back toward her, at this point we were both hanging onto these shoes. I can tell you something, there was no way I was letting go of those babies. As she spoke she pulled her way, as I spoke I pulled them my way.

I said, 'give me my shoes!' completely exasperated. Of course, a few people had stopped to look and listen. Then all of a sudden she lunges at me going for my face, when she missed that she tried to pull my hair. I duck back quickly just in time before she makes contact. Totally shocked. I see two people pounce on her and pull her back. Then Denise runs over asking what all this is about. All about! I feel like yelling at her.

Instead, I say, 'She is telling me these are her shoes, you and I both know these are my shoes and I need them. I need them right now. Please tell this woman that and get me back my shoes!' When she had lunged at me I let go of them.

Denise talks to the woman and hands me back my shoes. Then I go over to the table and quietly pick up everything on it and take it over and lay them all out in front of each look. As they should have been from the very start! That table was the most stupid, idiotic idea ever.

The manager says to me, 'Ok, you're up next, the models will be coming out in a minute, get ready!' Oh charming, I think to myself what a fabulous way to go into a show, I have just been in a cat fight with a crazy lady and nearly mauled. Thank goodness I still have my hair, and my face for that matter. If I had still had my lashes they would have been gone after that little fiasco. Just imagine if Tami had still been backstage, she would not have been able to believe her eyes. She thought it was crazy enough earlier. I really didn't even know how to prepare myself for what was ahead, as some of the models would be random ones that I've never fitted before and I am also going to have to fit them out with shoes, etc., in the space of like, thirty seconds... actually, maybe less.

Then I caught the designer's eye next to me who I helped out of her dilemma earlier. Who had promised to help me when it was my turn. I smiled at her and said, 'I am about to go on.' She just looks at me, then a few minutes later I see her take off out the back door. I could not believe it. I have always been brought up with, treat others as you want others to treat you. I would never dream of doing that to someone. She would not have gotten her collection on the runway, if it wasn't for me dressing all her models for her.

Ok well, here we go! Time for the big girl panties, cause it was show time and we are going to do this! The models start coming out and before I know it there are a bunch of models in front of me. I would have to say in the end, out of the fifteen, about five were ones I had actually fitted. The ones I had already fitted previously got their looks and started getting dressed to the point until they needed help. An assistant came over to help but the problem was all these new models I had never met were just looking at me.

'What am I wearing? What shoes go with this? I can't fit these shoes, what ones shall I wear? I can't get this dress on, it doesn't fit me'. Then Denise rushes over, seeing and knowing that I have basically almost a whole collection to instantly choose and fit. I was trying to keep calm and deal with one thing at a time but it was actually impossible as they were ALL at me. Even the assistant and Denise were asking me the same things, as of course they were trying to dress models and didn't know what went with what. The shoes were all mixed up and out of order. Again, I was so overwhelmed.

Take a deep breath girl I said to myself, mother's words once again in my head, 'it will come to pass'. Seriously though, is there even such a thing as a smooth show? Or is it just me?

So I thought, Ok just get them all dressed into something and then they can wait at the runway entrance behind stage and anything I need to adjust and fix, I can quickly try and do it in line as they are waiting to go on. That made me feel like I could manage better. It was a whirlwind and so many things I can't even describe. They all get dressed and then I take off to the front entrance where they have lined up. I work my way quickly giving each look a once over. Some have the wrong shoes, some have the design on the wrong way, and some have no accessories at all. I don't know how but I was running back and forth, from front to back and back to front getting what I could and shoving it on them. Then I have to stop.

I can't do anymore. Time's up! I step back and take a look at them all. Oh no, this order is all wrong! I apologize to them all at the start saying, 'I'm sorry if I am manhandling you but I just need to quickly shuffle some of you into the right spot as you are out of order.'

They were all pretty good about it and had a stressful time themselves trying to work with the chaos. They were literally like life-size chess pieces in my hands. I got them and moved them all into place. One goes here, one goes there, as I quickly maneuver them down the line. Done! Just as the first model walks out. I MADE IT. Even if they are a little hit and miss, the designs look fab!! Then the last model goes out and comes back to get me for the finale walk. By the way, I had only just remembered before the show started that I wasn't dressed so thankfully I had just put my dress on and was doing up my shoes when the models came out. My dress was cute and playful and very Lilika. It had a cream lace bodice with little cap sleeves, a collar and hot pink tie at the neck. The waistband and gathered skirt was in gold. The back had a big low scoop in full lace. Tami and Bevan were front row and right at the top end so I saw them as soon as I came out.

After the finale walk we all got back stage and everyone clapped and said how awesome the collection looked. Could I breathe now? Yes I could! Then Tami comes to the back giving me a big hug and saying how fabulous the collection looked on the runway.

She asked me, 'How did it all go back there after I left?'

'Sister you have NO idea, I will fill you in later!'

All of a sudden I felt shattered but had to get straight out the front to network and talk to everyone. Tami said she would stay back there and pack everything up. She did too, until the very end, she sat there and beautifully packed all the designs up, all the shoes, accessories everything. What a woman! I couldn't have faced doing all that right then. I am blessed to have some amazing friends in my life and also able to share some amazing experiences with them. This one was slightly more exhilarating than I had anticipated. These shows certainly don't disappoint for stimulation that's for sure. Wait till I tell Sheryl.

Before I had gone out front to Bevan, my very special young lady Emma had come back stage still in her dress from the runway. She had done a fabulous job walking and we could see her mum was super proud, and so she should be. It was backstage, during it all, that Tami had told me that she had spoken with her mother Maria, and tonight Emma was actually part of the Make A Wish Foundation. I hadn't any idea when I had first met them, it was all so busy and she had just been introduced to me as it was a dream for her to walk. I had made no connection whatsoever.

Anyway, back to backstage. I could see Emma didn't even contemplate taking the dress off. She was so in love with it. I decided that this dress belonged with this special girl, and said 'I want you to have this dress, I want you to remember this special night and Lilika.' She, her mum and Tami all burst into tears of happiness. She couldn't believe it that her princesses's dress was all hers to keep and to take home. I was happy that it had made them so happy. I gave them both a huge hug and we went out front and took some photos together. I had two nephews who went through the Make A Wish Foundation and remember how special it was for them to have one of their wishes become a reality. So it seemed even more fitting that I had this reality with Emma.

I kept in touch with them both after the show and still do to this day. We will definitely get to see each other again one day at another show I'm sure. They have also kindly invited Bevan and I to visit them in their holiday home in Capecod. I can't wait to see them again in the future.

Back out the front, I finally met up with Bevan, who gives me a hug and kiss. We had a great chat with everyone and met some awesome contacts in the industry. The feedback from the show was super positive and I had quite a few people come up to me saying how much they loved the collection. I did a couple more interviews and already had some meetings teed up and orders getting placed. After all the networking for some time, we went to a close by restaurant/bar with Tami for some much needed chill out. Sarah was also there with her film crew relaxing after a huge day. We said we would keep in touch with each other and we did. Not long after the show, when I was back home, she wore Lilika again. What a fab night it had been. We were meeting up with some of the crew after this.

By the time we got to the hotel it was the early hours of the morning but guess what? Tomorrow we could sleep in and then we would be heading off on our big roadie to San Diego, to meet my long lost family. Yippee. Now the holiday begins.

We woke after an awesome sleep to another crystal clear sunny day, everyday was the same. I know I sound like a stuck record but it was so beautiful here. California weather was definitely living up to its name. I could SO get used to this. New Zealand, and especially Auckland doesn't have the saying, 'four seasons in a day' for nothing.

After a delicious big breakfast and a large coffee, we walked back to our hotel. We packed up and got a ride to where we were picking up our rental car.

We had a huge amount of luggage as you can imagine with all the collection stuff. We had booked a standard sized car and thought that would be all we needed. Then as the taxi was unpacking all our cases, one after the other, after the other, we started to think. Hmmm, I hope all this is going to fit into the car we have booked.

We got talking to the nice guy at reception, he was fascinated with the Kiwi accent as many people seemed to be. He asked us what we had come to LA for and we told him.

'So you were actually a designer showing?'

'Yes, just last night was our show.'

Next thing we know he started typing on the computer.

After a couple of minutes, he said, 'Here we go, I think you will find this car way more suitable for you both, no extra charge'. He handed us the keys to the biggest SUV that was there, three times the size of what we had booked. It was big and black and awesome with tons of room for all our cases. 'Have a great trip and hopefully we will see you in LA for your next show'. That was pretty cool, thank you very much, you very nice man… we like you.

Off we go. We had already googled how to get on the motorway or the freeway as they call it there. With the Wi-FI from the hotel, and screenshots of the full route, just in case we needed it. We we would use the car GPS though. We had been told it was about two hours with no traffic.

Now let's just make one thing clear, we come from a country where our main highway has two lanes and our harbor bridge connecting the shore to the city has only three lanes on each side. Hundreds of thousands use the bridge everyday. The traffic is always so bad because of course there are so few lanes. SO you can imagine our panic when we turn onto the LA freeway that has not only heaps of lanes but a thousand on and off ramps. Then what looks like exits off the exit ramp, and signs everywhere. Oh man, this was ever so confusing.

Pleased I wasn't driving, I said to Bevan, 'Ok babe I think we need to put the GPS on now, this is crazy!'

'Yeah.' So we look around inside the truck. There is no GPS, we just assumed... 'Ummm... Houston we have a problem.'

Our GPS is not working on our phones and we have no GPS in the truck. HOW are we going to get all the way to SD, and out to where the family is on a country estate, driving on the opposite side of the road to what we are used to, along with all the multitude of signs and exits? It will be one thing if we find where they live, and it will be another if we get there and still be married at the end of it!

Driving and maps were the one thing that got both our hackles up. Bevan hates not knowing where he is going, and I hate reading maps and giving directions – not a good combo. This was going to be fun.

Ok after we had got over the shock of no GPS we decide we will just have to go off the screenshots we had taken the other day off Google. Thank goodness we had them. We would have to try and follow it but after looking at this freeway with so many exits and double exits and so many lanes, it would definitely be a challenge.

At this stage, we follow the screenshot maps on my iPad and actually find our way out of LA, which we were quite amazed by. We were, we thought about half way when we went past the exit we were meant to take. Oh, the feeling of horror we both had. All of a sudden we had to make decisions of what way to turn, then I see over to the right there is a ramp to get back on the freeway. I yell out, 'quick babe to the right, to the right!'

He just turned around in time, thank goodness, and we jumped back on. Phew, at least that hadn't been too bad, the ramp had been right there to get back on, we would't be so lucky if that happened again.

Now we are back on but in the other direction of course, so the screenshots were all leading the opposite way on the iPad, we had to now think backwards. Sheesh! Ok, so I call out the name of the next exit we need to get off. The problem is taking the "exit" just means you move into another whole freeway, then you have to take something off that. I see the name we are after at the last moment before we went past, nearly missing it for a second time.

Right, next step. I was sitting poised on the edge of my seat, grasping my iPad with these screenshots like the world was about to end. The worst thing was that everything changed so fast; the lanes, the exits, so many signs you didn't have time to relax for a single moment. We knew that if we lost our way that would be it. We would have no idea whatsoever where we would be. All we had were these screenshots but only of the route displayed. Here I was thinking the stress of the show was over.

I glanced over at Bevan. He was gripping the steering wheel, with white knuckles, looking over it ready to do whatever he had to in an instant. He looked like how I was - on the edge of my seat. The tricky thing was with the screenshots was I had to be super-fast, flicking to the next one at a moment's notice to try and locate where we were, all without missing any signs and turn offs. If we weren't so focused we would have laughed our heads off at the situation. Not having our phones working on the internet was just another whole level. This seemed to be another repeat of NY – what was it with me and phone on trips?

Anyway, so we had got off at that first exit with the name that was on the iPad but of course, then there were about four other lanes to choose from and more exits, and this is where it all went to custard. We couldn't see anything that was following on from that first one, we just have to pretty much guess the right direction. Yeah – nuh… we got off and carried along some road and had no idea where we were. We decided to drive until we saw some shops with a café. We would stop, grab a coffee, try and chill out for half an hour and have something to eat. We would use their Wi-FI and try and figure out where we were. Hopefully, we were even heading in the right direction of SD.

Not much further down the road, we see a shopping mall, with a café in the corner. We order our coffee, feeling almost like a whiskey at this point. We get the Wi-FI password and sigh a million times between us. The sun was shining outside, a gorgeous day for a roadie, just a shame about the way we were traveling, haha. The coffee was amazing and we got muffins to have with it, raspberry and white chocolate yum! Just what we needed, a pit stop, even if it was initially unwanted.

The owner was the loveliest guy, he asked us where we were from and we got chatting. We told him that we were actually lost and had got to this point with no GPS, just by screenshots. His mouth was hanging open, he could not believe that were driving from LA for the first time ever in California. He was impressed. He then showed us a map and told us we were definitely off track but not as bad as we thought. Of course, once we had got lost, our screenshot directions were no use to us and as we had no idea how to get back to them.

Bless his heart, he prints out the route for us then writes all the directions on paper, which was way easier for me to just read off instead of quickly flicking through the different screens, trying to find the right one in time for when Bevan needed to know where to turn.

We had actually done really well getting to where we had. So we talked with him for a little while, we finished our coffee, gave him a big hug and thanked him for helping us. We will never forget that guy. When we got home, we gave him the best review ever.

With it all clearly written out, we got back onto the freeway and were now headed back towards SD. We were on the edge of our seats again though, as things came up so quickly with many options with each one, we had to get it right the first time. That was my job. It was just so much easier with the printout. I don't know how I had done it that far with the iPad. We finally hit SD and started to wind our way out to Ramona where our family was.

As we got into the country estate, we high fived and just could not believe we had arrived. We were also super proud that we hadn't killed each other either, under the stress, we were a really great team. All the house numbers here are written on the footpath edge, which to us was really weird. At home we have it on the letterbox and that was it. So we had a couple of runs up and down their street before we found the right number. Woohoooo, I was about to meet my long lost family.

We pull into the drive behind a shiny black jeep. I see a little white haired head peep out the window, then a second later there she was at the door. My gorgeous Auntie Josie. Mum is always telling me how much I remind her of Auntie Josie. I hug her and kiss her dear face, not believing we are here. Then we see Donna's hubby Jose' come out of the garage. Giving each other a huge hug. Oh, how wonderful to finally meet him after hearing so much about him. Bevan is hugging Auntie then Jose', then we see all the dogs at the fence. This is a real dog house with all shapes and sizes and breeds, each one excited to see who is visiting. Auntie tells me Donna will be home soon, she is on her way home from work in the city. I can't wait to see her. We bring our things into our room, and then tell them both how we got there with no GPS. Wow… they were shocked.

We relax for a while, chatting away, filling them in on the trip, I pop into the bathroom just by the front entrance. When I am washing my hands I hear the dogs barking happily and running around. I unlock the door, open it up and there I come face to face with Donna, my beautiful cousin. We both just look at each other for a moment, both surprised we had just banged into each other like that, as she had just walked in the front door as I was coming out the bathroom door. After a moment of stunned silence, all that could be heard is shrieking and screaming, kisses noises, more squeals, then more kisses. How can you meet someone for the first time in your life and instantly, magically connect like you have known them forever?

The feeling was just like we had felt online but now standing in front of each other. Or should I say leaping around like frogs. This was just the best ever! The dogs are jumping up and down, everyone is all excited. Donna comes through to the living area, puts her bag down, meets and hugs Bevan for the first time. We decide to open a bottle of wine to celebrate. The stress of the show and the drive evaporates.

We have a wonderful dinner together all sitting in the back yard. It is magical, the view is amazing, we sit down on the outdoor couch in a beautiful courtyard area lit by candles and

Our first pic together.

Bevan and Aunty, he very quickly got nicknamed 'Cutie pie'.

Super happy me.

The guys Bevan and Jos'e.

sitting around a fire pit, the air is so lovely and warm and the sun was setting. The dogs were laying on the warm concrete. What a night.

We all talked till late, it was so lovely and we were relishing every moment of each other's company. My long lost family, how had I managed to spend my life so far without these gorgeous people in it? Lilika had brought us together. How had Donna and I never met? It was bitter sweet really, we both just kept saying at times over the stay, 'imagine if we had been able to be a part of each other's lives? Imagine this, imagine that.'

Even more now we could see for real how much we have missed out on. She was just like my sister, we were so totally on the same wave length with stuff. She was obsessed with shoes, bags, and clothes. The following night we spent half of it in her wardrobe! She has the most amazing closet stuffed full of the most delectable things. I was in heaven. I got excited enough doing all my looks for the Runway shows, this was another level. We had so much fun. But I've jumped forward a night. Back we go...

We finally say a happy but tired goodnight and go to bed. They had both taken the day off work the following day so we could have the day together, which was awesome. We went out like lights (the prettiest and blingiest, most divine chandeliers of course). It had been a huge week all around. Make that a huge three months.

We open the curtains to the most beautiful clear blue day (of course, what else would it be). I have a feeling of complete freedom. We don't need to be anywhere, we can do whatever we want. I have no people to dress but myself, no designers to fight off, no shoes to defend, and no face to protect. Ahhh, the bliss of just doing absolutely, zilch… nothing. I love California. I love my life.

After breakfast we head out on a roadie for the day, it was time to check out the sights of SD. On the way through Ramona, we pull up to a takeout looking place and turn into a drive-through. No way!! It was a drive-through Dunkin Donuts, they have a drive through donut shop. Sheesh, we were sounding like country bumpkins, but really? Bevan was in heaven as he adores donuts and his face was magic when he sees the big board of them all. Jos'e orders a box of all sorts and we would have been there all day deciding if it had been up to us. We are on our way munching on the donuts, lips covered in icing sugar as we drive into the city.

The landscape is so beautiful and rugged, the girls in the back and the boys in the front. We were also going

Donut time so delish!

Selfie with my gorgeous cousin Donna and Auntie Jos'e on the way into SD town.

My long lost family selfie.

Happy us.

Hanging out at Mission Brewery.

to meet their son Cody, who of course I had never met. He was head brewer downtown in SD. We had more of the family to meet on the weekend and I couldn't wait.

Our family had a strong navy background so we go down to the waterfront to see the frigates amongst everything else. The waterfront is gorgeous, I could so easily live here in a heartbeat.

We took tons of photos, had lots of laughs and many spontaneous hugs along the way, so happy to be together. Having Auntie there too from Vancouver was wonderful. She and Dad had been the naughty ones out of the six kids when young. I could just picture them both together, they have the same cheeky fun personality. To have this time with her was very special.

Bevan was loving it, everyone he meets loves him, he is so easy going and happy with a great sense of humor. It was cool to hear about all the family history. We even got to go through the naval base, which was amazing. Just to be in singlet tops and shorts felt so good, like we hadn't felt the sun on us in forever, after our very wet last couple of winters in NZ.

We then head over to the brewery and surprise Cody who had no idea we were coming. He was awesome, so was the brewery, where we sat up at the huge long bar and I had the best wine slushy ever, Bevan thoroughly enjoyed awesome cold beer. We got to choose some tshirts and very cool beer and shot glasses to take home. We were introduced to the most amazing chips I had ever eaten. Auntie loved them as much as me, they became our obsession while we were in SD after that… to the point one day after we get back home a box arrives in the mail full of our fav chips and goodies from Donna – it was soooo good. We had been missing them so much when we got home, we had only just found the other family members and then we had to leave them. Anyway the chips… best things ever.

Best wine slushy ever.

Chelsea, Auntie and me.

After hanging out there for a while we hop back in the car, and before heading home, go over to Coronado to do some more sightseeing. We then met their daughter Chelsea who was manager at a local café. She was just gorgeous and a real sweetie and just like her beautiful mum.

We sat down outside and had ice creams. By now it was late afternoon so we headed back home. We had had such a lovely day. We were meeting Chelsea, her fiancé Steve and kids, for dinner at the country club that night.

When we arrived back at the house, the dogs were excited to see us and they were like jumping jacks, from tiny to super big, it was so funny to watch. Each had their own personality and it was hard to pick a favorite. Bevan loves dogs and they could sense that, he had them all over him the whole time we were there. He had never owned his own dog when growing up. Whereas I had grown up surrounded by horses and German Shepherds.

Later on, we drive over to the beautiful country club, which wasn't too far from the house, and meet the others for dinner. Chelsea's fiancé Steve and Bevan hit it off like long lost brothers, and we got to meet the adorable super cute kids; Connor and Skyler. I had the most amazing dinner, the food was so good and the company even better. What an awesome day it had been, trying not to think about how awful it was going to be to leave them. They were all just SO us as people, there was an easy, enjoyable, fun connection that is hard to come by and definitely not always one that comes from just being blood relations.

After saying good night to the others, we head home for a lovely soak and wine in the hot tub, in the beautiful warm country air outside in the courtyard. Bliss.

The next morning Donna and Jose' had work so we had the day with Auntie all to ourselves. I am treasuring any time I have with her. We decided we would head up to the little old mining town Julian for the day. It wasn't too far from the house and Bevan was our driver for the day, nicknamed 'James' by Auntie. We sat in the back in true style while he drove us. It was a super-hot day, the town was the prettiest little place. So quaint and loaded with history, we just love places like this.

We shopped all morning and stopped for a yummy lunch that finished with a hot fresh apple pie, shopped some more, then back in the car for James to take us home. We were all ready for a siesta.

Us.

We were still chilling out in the lounge with our feet up when Donna and Jos'e got home from work. Auntie was in 'her' big comfy chair in the corner with the tiniest dog Sophie on her lap. The other dogs sprawled all over the place on the cold tiles. Bevan was sitting on the huge leather couch with me. I was happy and content, enjoying every bit of it.

Another evening of wonderful company, food and wine.

While the boys were hanging out together, Donna and I decided to take our lovely glasses of red and hang out ourselves. In the most fun and awesome room in the house – Her closet. Did I really even need to say? Yip. There we were, buried amongst the drawers, the shelves, the racks, it all. Oh my, what a wonderous little happy place I was in and with my beautiful cousin. We dressed up, we rummaged, we drank, and we laughed. I'm sure the squeals and the laughs and the thumping around in there could clearly be heard from outside.

Auntie in 'her chair' with her little buddy.

After our glasses were empty and my feet were aching, from clip clopping around in all the magnificent designer shoes we collapse on the bed happily. By now it was the wee hours of the morning and time to head for the glorious sheets and the feather filled pillows. With kisses we said goodnight.

It was Saturday tomorrow and we were having a family get together with everyone at Cody's and his wife Zulma's place. They have a ton of dogs, even more than here. Can't wait to meet everyone.

I checked my emails before bed. I had been starting to get all the photos through from the show and they were stunning. It already felt like some time ago. The collection looked so good, and the models I ended up with looked fab. We had already talked with a showroom here in the US who was keen to take on Lilika, so that was awesome. It was so funny how the brand was getting introduced internationally before its own home country. Another showroom in the UK would take on the brand there too.

Remember, I mentioned earlier Lilika had been asked to feature in Cosmopolitan over there and the magazine was due out soon? I opened up my emails to a US magazine, wanting to feature Lilika with a full page. They felt that the brand would be a great fit for their glossy fashion magazine. Once I was home I would send them through some images to see what fitted with their aesthetic best. Wow… that was awesome.

So a few times a day I would jump online and answer any emails and keep things up to date. We had already been asked back for the next season's show. We would see how everything was tracking when we got home. I had a feeling that I would once again hit the ground running, and fast.

I checked in back home with Mum, Dad, and the kids. They were all well and happy and excited that the show had gone well, and that we were now finally relaxing. Time to power off as my eyelids were heavy, with the feeling that toothpicks were needed. Goodnight beautiful people.

You guessed it, another perfectly clear blue day with the sun shining. Cali totally rocks! Donna and I met up with Chelsea to take the dogs for a walk. The walk was so rocky and rugged that it reminded me of the South Island back home. I don't know if we took the dogs for a walk or if they took us, either way, we were all pretty tired when we got back.

We would see Chelsea later for the family dinner starting later this afternoon. I absolutely love baking whenever I have the time, so decided I would make some super yummy carrot muffins with cream cheese icing to take for after dinner tonight. They were a favorite back home. Everybody seems surprised when I tell them Bevan always has fresh baking in his lunch for work everyday. I don't know if it is because they just assumed I wouldn't do things like baking, or because I CAN actually bake. I have always had such a sweet tooth and it, without a doubt was handed down to me from Dad. It's a wonder Bevan gets the full batch. It's a little like, one for you… three for me.

Back to the kitchen. When the carrot muffins were made, it was hang out time. Before we knew it though, the time had rolled around to leave. We all piled into the car and off we went. Family time – nothing better.

Not too long after we pull up outside, walk into the house and the amazing smells wafting from the kitchen hit us. I am introduced to Zulma, a beautiful dark haired girl that happens to be Cody's wife. They got married not long before us and had the same wedding colors and wedding song. Great minds think alike. She is full of life and a darling. Then I meet a very close family

Snuggles up on the beach with Aunty.

The boys, Steve and Bevan.

friend, Alex, along with all the dogs that are outside with the rest of the family by the pool. Before long, Bevan was in the pool along with the dogs. Where there was water, there was Bevan.

I have now officially met all of the family in SD. We had the most wonderful time together, all piled around a big long table that was covered with delicious food. Lots of talking and laughing. Bevan introducing them all to the "Kiwi shot" that involved strategically placed lime. Tears of laughter and possibly a little pain. A time we will never forget. I was totally head over heels in love with my family.

The time went so fast and before long we were saying our goodbyes until the morning. We had all arranged to meet out at the beach for a surf (Bevan and Chelsea's fiance Steve), then we would all have breakfast together for the last time at the café on the waterfront. It was Bevan's first surf in Cali and he loved it, with his new found "bro".

We all sat on the beach with nice hot coffees and watched them surf. I was nestled up to Auntie on the blanket and we had also snuck our fav chips into our bags that we were munching away on.

A little while after, the boys came in from the surf and we walked over to the beachfront café, pretty hungry at this point. Even if Auntie and I had been scoffing the chips.

After a beautiful breakfast and with lots of hugs and kisses, we said our goodbyes. All of us wished we had more time together. We were driving back to LA tonight as we were booked into a hotel ready for our early morning flight home. We didn't want to get stuck in traffic on a Monday morning heading into LA.

After we got back to the house and were welcomed gleefully once again by all the dogs, we just laxed out happily. The afternoon went by so fast, and once again before we knew it, the

Family (with Donna on the camera).

time had come to pack up and load the truck. There was SO much luggage, of course, this time going back we had all the collection with us too.

We ended up leaving a box of Runway shoes at Donna's as we were so far over in weight already it was crazy. We would get them when we were back for the next show. We were all determined to keep in touch and not lose each other again – there had already been too many wasted years. It was a good excuse to come back. Bevan loaded it all into the truck and I was checking in my bag we had our passports etc., opening up the passport wallet, yip there was mine and ……looking and looking…I can't find Bevan's anywhere.

He walks in at that moment and I say to him, 'Babe, did you put your passport somewhere else cause it isn't with mine like normal?'

Trying to keep the slight panic out of my voice. He looks at me, like just staring then slowly I see his face change.

'OH NO you have got to be kidding me?' We all just look at him … It is in LA in the hotel, I left it in the hotel room.'

Ahhhhhhhh, ya did what? The hotel room that we checked out of a week ago? Here come the little hammers in my temples, I can feel them.

Then he says, 'But don't worry, cause I know where it is… I hid it.' Ummm, ok, is he losing the plot or what? We all just stare at him.

'Well the last time we were heading out that day I didn't want to take it with me and so I thought I would just hide it somewhere in there, well I forgot all about it!' Ahh and the safe is normally for what, may I ask?

Ha ha… oh dear… I could see he was kicking himself to the curb and back for leaving it there, no point in giving him grief about it. I looked at Donna and she looked shocked.

They were saying, 'But that means you will have to go back into downtown LA tonight to get it, then over to your new hotel by the airport?' Oh sheesh, I hadn't thought of that.

Ok well it is what it is, the one thing I was very thankful for was at least he knew where it was! Hopefully, we could get back into our old room as I know there were people coming in after us – there is never a dull moment.

After tears and lots of tight hugs we pulled out of the driveway and waved goodbye to our beautiful little family. Auntie was eighty-one years old, and I was so happy and thankful I got to have that time with her and that she was able to especially come over to be with us during our stay. She was heading home herself in the morning. I have always believed everything in life happens for a reason and if I got nothing else out of my brand, it found me my family again and I will be forever grateful for that.

Jose had printed out a map with directions to take us straight to our hotel and then from the hotel to the airport in the morning. So we were all good to go. It was so sad to leave them behind but so happy we had the time with them. We were almost at LA when Bevan notices that the gas is very low. Oh dear we were so busy just following our directions to get out of SD so we had no issues we had forgotten to fill up with gas. Sheeeesh… I could tell he looked pretty worried and after looking at the dial, said there is no way we have the gas to reach much further.

All of a sudden we had to look for an exit as fast as we can, and get over all the lanes to get to it. Also, we were hoping it was easy enough to get back onto it once we had got our gas. The numbers on the dial were rapidly declining and we had got off the exit but now trying to find a station.

After going through a couple of sets of lights, right there on the main road was a gas station. Yay, we will make it. After filling up with gas we go back the way we had come. Bevan pulls out into the main road then all we see are cars coming right towards us!

'Ahhhhh… baby cars… You are on the wrong side quick get off!!'

He puts his foot on the accelerator and thank goodness a side street is right there so he shoots into it and pulls over. Okaaaay, that was close. Another dilemma overcome. We get back out onto the main road turning onto the correct side of the road this time.

We follow our way back and jump back on the freeway towards LA. Getting closer into the city we thankfully are able to make our way back into downtown and then a few places become familiar and we find our hotel. The guy was very surprised to see us back again, to say the least. We tell him about our little issue and he informs us that there are people in the room staying but not currently at this moment as they went out an hour or so ago. I think he found it quite amusing that Bevan had hidden it so well he forgot about it. He said he will take them in some extra towels and Bevan could come with him to quickly get the passport.

Five minutes later he comes out with passport in hand. PHEW, we can actually fly home tomorrow. Off we go again.

It was a smooth ride after that and we found our hotel. After checking in we crashed, setting the alarm for really early. Whilst talking to the hotel manager, he said we need to leave super early to avoid the morning rush hour traffic in to the airport. We were leaving the truck there so that was easy. It only felt like an hour later before we hear the awful ringing of the alarm.

Shortly after, like zombies, we hop back into the truck. The traffic was good and only a little sticky closer to the airport. Getting there in plenty of time to check in we went for a wander around duty free and relaxed until boarding.

We had a great flight back home, with no issues, stopping in Hawaii again on our way for a couple hours. We had coffee and something to eat then caught our connecting flight. We were on the last leg of the trip.

I don't know what it is, but I just cannot sleep on planes. It is so frustrating. So I used the time to write and sketch instead. Bevan watched movies and slept. Lucky him.

We touch down on time in Auckland – Kiwi land. What an awesome, mad and amazing trip. Another journey to add to my "belt".

Whenever we go away we drive our car to the airport and park it with one of the yards that look after the cars while people are travelling. They pick you up from the airport in their van and the depot is just a few minutes down the road. You pick up your car and go from there. It has been a long flight and we were super tired, and just wanted to be home. It was late evening here.

We hop in the van and he asks for our names. All he says is, 'ohhh… so you are the ones, where have you come from?' We tell him, he then says, 'we have a problem with your car…..'

Are you kidding meeee… what now?!

'One of the guys who was on the prior shift didn't bring your car over in time from the carpark over there (pointing next door) before it got locked down. Now it's all padlocked up and we can't get it out till tomorrow'.

Silence. This has got to be the last thing we feel like. See what I mean about just attracting situations? I was dead on my feet and just wanted my car, a shower and my bed, in that order.

Bevan and I look at each other.

The guy says, 'there are two options'. Oh wonderful I think, aren't we lucky. 'First one, we put you up here in a motel for the night, and in the morning we get your car out and you can drive home. The other option is you take this van back home and I will get a ride up to you after my shift in the morning and pick the van back up'.

Bevan replies, 'Yip, we will take the van mate, we will be sitting in traffic for hours trying to get home if we go in the morning, even though we are so tired right now a motel sounds good, but yeah-nuh.'

We grab the keys, load all our luggage back into the van and get going. We are nearly home when I have a sudden realization and turn around and count the bags in the back. Oh no. This is a time I don't want to be right. We have forgotten a bag. One of my bags. There had been something niggling at the back of my mind but I just couldn't think what it was. We had traveled the whole way to LA with our set amount of bags but of course on the way back we had to take an extra one back with the collection in it. We had been used to checking our normal number, so when we were collecting our bags after arriving in Auckland. We counted our normal set of bags then left. Leaving behind the extra one. I break the news to Bevan. We are almost at home now so we would have to drive back over tomorrow (oh the joy) and pick up our lonely bag that had been completely ditched. I imagined it going round and round the carousel for quite some time. Oh well. At least we forget it in NZ and not the US.

We pull into our drive, SO happy to be home. Park in the garage and just forget everything else, and climb into bed. Ahhhh our own bed. Sleep we did.

Update: in the following couple of months since we have been home from LA, we have been asked to feature again in *Cosmopolitan* for the second time. Then came a third of a page in *Harper's Bazaar* collector's issue, followed by a quarter page in *ELLE*. Invitation to *Milan Fashion Week, Paris, London, New York* and more. So let's just say things are certainly happening. Not too bad for a little Kiwi brand. Right? Our posh, perfect and pretty little monster.

There is so much more that is already going on that I want to share with you as I am still writing this book, but you will have to wait for another time.

Or maybe I can just sneak one thing in…some time after the dust had settled I was approached by these cool guys from, oh, just a little old place called Beverly Hills in that postcode you probably don't know..90210? (Couldn't resist) and they just have a gorgeous celebrity Haute Couture designer boutique inside the golden triangle. You know the one at Rodeo Drive? Yes that part of the world. They also have their own fabulous award winning TV show which is filmed at their boutique. Yes, soooo… well they contacted me and told me, they would love to have Lilika hanging on their racks…so she kind of has a new home but you will have to wait for all the rest. I know I have another book, or five in me!

Oh, and I just know there is more for Lilika, just around the corner. I can't wait to see what delicious opportunities come to me. I will design more beautiful clothes for you lovely people, there will be more doors to throw wide open and bolt through. More of it all. Totally in love and obsessed with my wonderful life.

Lilika's "Manoula" dress sitting pretty on screen, while filming the TV show in the Beverly Hills boutique with Pol and Patrik.

Pol and Patrik's award winning TV show, Gown and Out in Beverly Hills.

Passion, Fashion & Heart

Moments

Here are just a few of my moments, some favorite snaps, my loves, that rock my boat, that make me shine and that forever move me forward. From my fashion obsessed journey and those connected to it, the people closest to me in my life and of course that big handsome furry dude- nicknamed the gentle giant-my horse Atlas. One word - Blessed

Passion, Fashion & Heart

Christina Kilmister

Passion, Fashion & Heart

Christina Kilmister

Woman are beautiful and individual, so it's important that you wear the right clothes for your body. Bring out that inner goddess, that rock star chick, whoever maybe hiding in there, and let her rule. Wear that crown.

Do you need to drape, do you need to accentuate or do you need to elongate? What do you need to do? Yes, it can be overwhelming, just like Emma felt at the start. But she got it sorted, and so can you.

You can obtain the most beautiful clothes in the world, but if you don't know what to wear and how to wear them, you are not doing your body justice. You are not giving the clothes the opportunity to come alive on your body, the way they should. Refine and define your body, embrace it, so you can feel fabulous, inside and out.

Earlier on I gave you some brief facts on each of the ladies body types. You will now get more detailed information on each shape, which in turn, will give you an idea of your own body shape. What clothes should be gracing your body and which should never touch your body. You will learn when to say yes I want that in every color. When to throw it wildly out of your closet and heave that puppy into the dump.

We have just focused on the five shapes, yes there are more shapes in the sense of you may be in between two of the shapes, you maybe a pear with a big bust, you could be an hourglass with small bust. I wanted to stick to the five simple shapes, which will give you a very good idea on what shape is yours. To the point you will know what to wear and what not to wear. I don't want you to get too caught up with too many shapes and images, just choose the closet to your shape and go from there. I want this to be an easy fun process not a confusing stressful one!

Right gorgeous ladies, let's get started!

The Apple – The Mandy

This body shape of the Apple is best described as round. Your waist is not defined and is your widest part. You don't have to have a very large tummy to be an Apple, it just means that is where your extra weight resides. You have a flatter bottom and your shoulders tend to be broad. You have thinner arms and legs and your hips are narrower than your bust.

With Apples you are likely to have great boobs, so make use of them, keep the focus up top, rather than down below. Showing off your bust not only emphasizes one of your greatest features, it draws the eye away from the middle area. We need to lessen your tummy's impact on the rest of your frame. The first step for apples is to get a great fitting bra. You need clear definition between your bust and your tummy. This will make all the difference.

Fabulous parts of the Apple – your boobs.

Dressing an Apple

No you can't – upper deck

- High necklines, no tops that cover your chest area, we need to open that up and show expanse.
- Large shapeless tops that don't show any waist. Keep it more straight lined and very slightly fitted, just nothing that hangs square.
- Heavy bulky jackets that just add volume to your upper half. No lapels, double breasted coats and jackets. Don't wear belts, big or small. They will not flatter you.
- Stay away from detail, added bulk, excessive fabric, tiers, gathers, ruching around the bust, waist and tummy areas. Keep any detail above the bust line and below the hip line. In between those lines keep it plain and simple so as to not draw the eye to that area.
- Don't wear sleeves that finish near your bust line.

Yes you can – upper deck

- Flattering draping/flowing fabrics yet still with some shape, not ones that hang square. Straighter lines.
- Tops that are tight under the bust, that highlight your body at the slimmest part, which is often just under the breast line and length that finishes just below the hip line.
- Wear V-neck tops and basically any tops that open you up at the chest area.
- Shirts also look best when they are fitted just underneath the bust and then flare out.
- Also try to get the V-shape happening with your shirts. Again we want to see skin up top.
- Dresses should have their waistline just below the bust. Baby doll style is great. A-line dresses also elongate your body and draw attention upstairs.
- Patterns and prints look fab on an Apple shape body as they flatter and camouflage all at once. Do not wear a completely different band of print or pattern just around the tummy area or again you will look straight there even if it is still patterned.

- Straight lapel jacket or cardigan with V-shape at top – we want to confuse and deceive the eye. Try wearing a straight lapel jacket or cardigan open over a fitted shirt. This creates three distinct portions through the middle of your body, each long and slim. Elongating your frame.

- A straight cut coat that ends just above the knee will create a nice long silhouette.

- Tops with detail above the bust line that draws attention there and confuses the eye.

Yes you can – lower deck

- Think plain and simple for the tummy and hip area.

- Get trousers that have zippers at the side to avoid adding extra bulk on the front. We don't want any clinging to the tummy or thighs. Avoid pleats if you can but if there are pleats they must be below the belly line.

- Choose jeans that have a great cut and are either straight or flared.

- Choose skirts that have their zippers at the side. Structured pencil skirts work well, but keep them at knee length. Don't go above knee length.

- Make sure that any pleats of skirts or dresses start below the belly to avoid adding extra volume.

No you can't – lower deck

- High waisted trousers and pants with chunky zips and pockets at the front.

- No waistbands.

- Keep your skirt/dress length knee or below.

- No detail and volume around tummy and hip area. Once again, plain and simple is the key.

- No pleats in the tummy area.

- No belts on waist or hip, big or small.

Shoes:

- A small shaped wedge is a great heel for you – it works well in showing off your slim ankles, while giving you good support at the same time. It also avoids any unnecessary contrast between the size of your upper body and the slenderness of your lower legs. Avoid kitten and petite heels. Boots also don't flatter.

- For evening wear, choose a higher and sexier heel in the same wedge shape.

The Strawberry – The Jayne

This body shape has a generous bust, wide shoulders, longer legs and narrow waist and hips. Basically, your lower half is smaller than your top half. Your shoulders are wider than your hips. These are the defining features of the Strawberry. Also known as the Inverted Triangle or the Lollipop.

Balancing the figure and de-emphasizing the broadness up top are the keys to this shape. We need to accentuate the lower body while gently softening the upper body, especially the shoulders.

This means you need to subtly broaden the hips and also accentuate the waist, to take away the look that can be too top heavy. You need to look at styles that even out your figure a little, to make the proportions balanced. A great fitting bra that sits and lifts correctly is a must. The key for this shape is really to create visual balance.

Fabulous parts – your legs!

Dressing the strawberry

No you can't – upper deck

- Polo neck or high neck tops/sweaters, no boat neck styles.
- No details and added volume on your shoulders, for example, no puff sleeves, gathers or shoulder pads.
- No oversized collars or lapels.
- Stay away from bold patterns on top, it will just make you look wider. No horizontal stripes.
- Chunky knitwear will make you look top heavy, so steer clear of it. Just think – no bulk upstairs.
- Don't wear anything that hangs loosely from the bust. Shift dresses are not flattering to your shape. Don't wear styles that hide your silhouette.

No you can't – lower deck

- Avoid flat fronts
- Stay away from a cut that is too tight or skinny, as you are in danger of looking too top heavy. No tapered in skirts.

- Also don't wear very wide leg pants as they can make your legs look like sticks and unnaturally thin. Plus you hide those fabulous legs. The more bootleg style that flares our gradually toward the hem line, the best for your shape.
- High waist pants and skirts do not work well.

Yes you can – top deck

- Scoop neck tops – along with deep V-necks, are an essential part of your wardrobe, preferably in knit fabrics.
- Square and sweetheart necklines also work. Basically, we are after some expanse up top. Nothing closed up. Show us some skin.
- Wear tops that are nipped in at the waist, with banding or wrap style tops and finish just on the hip bone. A little flare at the bottom of tops and jackets is great, adds curve to the hips.
- With the said necklines it will open up and take the focus off your shoulders whilst the rest of the top will hug your waist and emphasize your curves. What is not to love?
- A wide neck jacket or coat is great, again we are opening up that neckline. It is a must for anyone with a big bust. So make sure the jacket or coat has wide lapels. Buttons underneath the breasts, particularly two buttons nip it in beautifully as you're so slender everywhere else. This will accommodate your bust whilst drawing attention to your small waist. Wear jackets open to create a vertical line.
- Wear darker colors on top and textures that have a light look to them, to soften the shoulder line.
- Wear crop jackets where the hem line sits on the waist. The horizontal line will further emphasize the waist.
- Balloon sleeves help create curves in areas that have less.
- Peplum styles are fab as they create an illusion of hips, details on the hips work well. Balancing out that top half and focusing on the waist.
- Wear belts, they are wonderful for accentuation the waist.

Yes you can – lower deck

- Wear bright colors
- Wear full skirts

- Gathered dresses are perfect for your shape.
- The most subtle weapon is that waist. It is fabulous so work with it.
- You can wear belts or dresses with defined waistbands to draw attention to that small waist with your torso curving into it from above and below.
- Wear a dress that opens up your chest so your bust doesn't look trapped and suffocated, it will again emphasize your waist. Other than your bust you don't have a lot of curves going on.
- Draped fabrics are really good as they will adore and hug your hips, creating curves.
- An alternative is to cinch in the waist using the buttons of a jacket and if you are brave enough you can even go for a crop top and bare the midriff.
- The perfect skirt for this body shape is an A-line as it flares out from your hips. Creating an overall balance.
- Fluted/Tulip skirts are a great subtle means of creating a curve. Your slender legs will still look great but there is now some bulk below the waist.
- Pleated skirts also add volume below the waist in a gorgeous way. The pleats will help the skirt to move and fall in a manner that is chic and sophisticated.
- Bold prints and textures can also be effectively used to draw the eye down, you can also wear plain black on top as a slimming contrast. Horizontal stripes will make the lower half look wider.
- Wear trousers / pants that are mid to low rise and if you can with some detail at the hip. Pockets and embellishments at the front for added bulk (in a good way). Flap pockets work well.
- Pockets at the back can create an illusion of more volume on your butt. Even though this may seem outrageous to other shapes of talking about adding volume. For the Strawberry though, it balances out your body.
- Boot leg jeans and trousers with a slight flare below the knee, subtly create curves. The hems of the trousers will balance out your upper body and you'll look impossibly tall and curvaceous. Oh yes, we love that!
- Jeans with whiskering at the hips are great.

Shoes

- Slim / stiletto heels are fab for your shape – your calves are slender so a thin heel looks perfectly in proportion. Go bold and eye-catching with your footwear.

The Pear – The Emma

It's always all about finding balance between your top and your bottom. For the Pear, just keep the focus on your lovely slim top and the rest will naturally follow.

The key to remember here is thighs.

The Pear may look like she has got wide hips but actually, it's the thighs where the width is. Basically, your lower body is wider than your upper body.

To create that body balance, you will need to take emphasis away from the thighs/hips and draw it to the top half of your body. We want to add volume to the shoulders and upper body. Your bottom is rounded and your waist is well defined.

You can do this easily by just choosing tops with the right style and shape and also picking bold designs and colors. You can have fun with the upper deck so go all out and get creative and find your own personal style.

Now, the area below the knee we really need to draw outward and elongate that central part. Choose visually interesting hemlines that are wider, this will balance out the hip/thighs area, also making it appear slimmer. The hi-low styles would be great.

Usually Pear shaped ladies have narrower shoulders and a smaller bust in comparison to the waist and lower half of the body. Of course, you will need a great fitting bra, that goes without saying.

Fabulous parts of the pear – your shoulders and torso.

Dressing the pear

No you can't – lower deck

- Avoid short, tight skirts and pencil skirts, as they emphasize those problematic areas along the hips and thighs.

- Avoid clingy materials because these will just define the hips and thighs we would like to minimize.

- Bright colors on the lower half draw the eye, and you want to draw the eye somewhere else. Go with darker colors on the lower half and bring interest to the upper half to give balance.

- A skinny jean is going to hug every inch of your legs and the issue here is that it's hugging every inch of your legs! These are the least flattering for your shape.

- Avoid light, pale and "washed look" jeans. Especially ones that have the worn look around the upper leg and body section, as this will draw the eye to this area.

- Stay away from bias cut skirts. They are designed to highlight the hips by draping themselves all over them. This may be wonderful for another shape but for you they're going to be highlighting your thighs. We don't want that.

Yes you can – lower deck

- Wear darker colors on your lower body. This gives a slimming effect and isn't distracting.

- Remember not to highlight your lower half, in fact really minimize here. Keep things super simple.

- Hems of pants, skirts, and dresses need to be wider to balance out the hip / thighs.

- A-line skirts (longer length) and wrap dresses are great for Pears because they skim over those lovely curves without making them look unshapely. The clever weapon in working with your lower half is the wider leg pants. Or the straighter leg with a flare at the bottom half to create a full volume all the way to the bottom. These wider leg styles are your best option. It confuses the eye into thinking your thighs are thinner than they are and your legs are longer. Pants and jeans that are equal width or a little wider in the calf and ankle area, draw the eye away from the hip / thigh area.

- Pants and skirts that are flat-fronted or softly pleated will emphasize your smaller waist area.

- Visually interesting hemlines for skirts, pants and dresses are great, as this balances out the hip/thighs area making it appear slimmer.

- Wear the hi-low styles, these are also super comfy as well as looking fab on your shape.

- Tulip style would also work well.

- For jeans, choose darker shades of denim that will give more of a slimming effect.

- For pants and skirts wear darker blues, dark grays, blacks, browns and olive green – these are the best shades to work with. They will also go with most shirt colors.

- Jeans with fading below the knee can also work well for you. Again bringing the eye downwards.

Yes you can – upper deck

- Be fun and get creative with the tops you wear. You will find that it is difficult to go wrong when choosing tops with color, detail, and pattern that will draw the eyes upwards. So have fun, especially with the neckline, which is perfect for that added detail.

- Think embellishments with beading and collars. Scarves are great. Remember we want to highlight this upper half.

- Choose wider necklines, like boat neck, squared, sweetheart, V-neck or cowl to show off the neckline and shoulders. Show us the skin.

- Try some ruffles on the top (yes you are allowed). Also layering works.

- Jackets should be just above the waist and coats follow the same rule as the tops, the length of the coat can be either waist length or three quarter, this length will nicely cover your less than flattering areas.

- A belted coat with a structured skirt will emphasize your small waist, add volume to your upper half and deceive the eye about the shape of your lower half.

- Try something with some detail on the shoulder, this can work well here. Also, a pattern or detail to the bust and cuff area of the coat is great. Double breasted coats will give a fab balanced look. They also have such an elegant look about them.

- Add a shrug or cropped jacket to that strapless dress to attract more attention to your upper half. Because it finishes just under your breasts, it highlights the bust as well, again making your upper half look wider.

- Tops should be fitted and not baggy and should finish at the top of your waist to emphasize your well-defined waist.

- Invest in a good push-up bra to give yourself the oomph you need to show off that fabulous shape.

- For you Pears, the key when it comes to buying that perfect dress is to draw all the attention up top, you should show off your lovely arms, back, and bust.

- Strapless dresses with a generous skirt will look great on you, if you don't feel daring enough to show all that skin try a halter neck. They are fitted up top, which will show off your waist. Dresses with spaghetti straps will give your shoulders a slightly broader appearance and help balance you out.

No you can't – upper deck

- Avoid tops and jackets that end at your bottom because these draw the eye to your middle section, which we do not want to highlight.
- Don't wear baggy square tops that don't define your waist.
- Don't wear high necklines that cover up all the chest area.

Shoes

- Pointy toed shoes elongate the legs, so go for them.
- A straight boot will hide wider calves, and can look stylish and classy with almost anything.
- A thin stiletto and delicate heel is not a good idea as it will make them look bigger again. This doesn't mean you need to give up heels, just go for a chunkier one.
- Heels with an ankle strap just cut the leg off, making it look shorter, the straps have the same effect as the stiletto. There are plenty of options out there in your best suited style so don't worry about that.

The Pillar – The Georgie

Pillars are generally taller and have shoulders the same size as their hips, slim waists and long legs. Also known as the Column.

They don't have broad shoulders but their busts are the same width as their hips. They don't have much in the way of a waist, tummy or bottom.

The Pillar body shape is very much straight up and down. The key to making Pillars look their best is to try to introduce a little shape and emphasize or create curves.

Pillars are really to be envied, as very easily, they can look super. It doesn't take much at all. You need to create the illusion of hips, bust and end of waist areas.

The real issue is that your curves can disappear by simply being stretched out over your long frame. The best way to bring those curves back is to use blocks of color. In that way, you can make gorgeous use of your long legs, arms, and body without ending up looking like a Pillar. Avoid anything that is shapeless and hangs straight up and down.

Key for your shape – add curve. Just define and highlight that waist and you are good to go.

Fabulous part of the Pillar – gorgeous tall lean frame.

Dressing the Pillar

No you can't – upper deck

- Anything shapeless, particularly long coats, jackets, and dresses. We don't want any baggy styles that just hang from the shoulders. No double breasted jackets.

- Straight dresses in one block color does not flatter your shape, a Pillar is straight up and down, so wearing a dress that's straight up and down just emphasizes that exact fact. You will have no shape at all. Not good.

- Cropped tops are not a good style for you, your body is long and so are your legs. So all it will do is shorten the length of your body, which is then added onto the length of your legs, resulting in them looking out of proportion.

- Don't wear boxy jackets – they will emphasize the straight up and down of your torso.

- Long straight fitted sleeves don't work well. We want to create a roundness.

- Avoid square necklines on tops and dresses.

- No bulky and heavy textures.

Yes you can – upper deck

- Round necklines are great for you, as it softens the straight Pillar lines. A round neck line or a V-neck adds a touch of elegance.

- You look great in any length sleeve, sleeveless tops also show off your lean arms. The fluted and flared sleeve is the best option to add a little shape and avoid the straight up and down look.

- You have the perfect shape for a shirt but the best option is going to be something that breaks up the long expanse of your torso. Look for something that is textured and gathered at the waist to give you some curve.

- Angular shapes are great for the Pillar, especially if every line points to the middle.

- Strategically placed lapels or pockets, flared or with sleeves, pointed hemline, fitted waist with single button fastening, or belts, do that exact thing. The idea of the single button jacket is to breakup your torso, which the single button does, kind of like drawing a target there and defining it.

- Belted three-quarter length coat with hip pockets are perfect, as the length shows off the legs, the belt and hip pockets add curves and defines the waist.

- Wear accessories and keep them big, bold and as a statement to the outfit to add shape. Avoid anything too thin or long.
- Add shape with detail, a belt or peplum style is fab as it will give you great curves.
- Use layering to shorten the longer top half of your body.

No you can't – lower deck

- Don't wear a dropped waist, as it makes the legs shorter but also makes the torso look un-naturally long.
- Avoid full length block colors.
- Stay away from anything shapeless that just hangs straight up and down.
- Avoid long straight fitted lines in pants and dresses. We want roundness.

Yes you can – lower deck

- Highlight that waist. Accentuate it, nip it in.
- Wear high or low waisted styles, which veer to your waist.
- Highlight your hips and bottom by using pockets and pleats. Remember we want to create visual curves.
- Although you can wear practically any shaped pant the best idea is to go for one with a slight flare to add a little curve to your body. Break up and show off those super long Pillar legs. Cropped style also works well for you.
- An A-line skirt does the same job as a slight flare on the trousers, drawing attention to their curves. Choose a gently flaring A-line to give your lower half some shape. Mix up colors and patterns and have fun working out your own personal style.
- A bias cut dress, usually in chiffon, clings to every curve. The Pillar is perfectly shaped to pull it off.
- Choose something with floaty sleeves that will utilize your long arms. This example works so well because it will draw attention to your tiny waist, and the different blocks of color will further break up your long body.
- Fitted angular style dresses look great.

Shoes

- The heel should not be too thin, not too thick, just perfectly balanced. What matters is that you feel comfortable and supported. Other than that, you can get away with any style shoe. Flats are as good as heels for you.

The Hourglass – The Alice

The Hourglass shape is all about those womanly curves.

Your bust and hips are well balanced and you have a beautifully defined waist.

Your upper body is proportionate in length to your legs, which are shapely. Your waist is small in comparison to your hips and bust.

The key to dressing an Hourglass body type is to proportionally dress the top and bottom of your body while accentuating your waist.

All an hourglass woman needs to do is dress in clothes that follow the curves of her body shape, it's simply a case of realizing you have nothing to hide and accentuating everything you have.

Fabulous part of the hourglass – your super little waist.

Let me now tell you, this is my body shape so all you hourglass women out there… I get ya ladies…I feel ya! Years ago I really struggled with trying to figure out my shape, what I could wear and what I couldn't. Realizing that some of the things I loved to wear, I really shouldn't be wearing and vice versa. That was the hardest but once I just embraced my shape and came to the conclusion that this is my body. There is no swapping, exchanging, getting a refund, this is me and this is what I have. I will be grateful for my body. So I will learn all about it and wear the best possible clothes that flatter me and make me feel unstoppable. I did, and now I love my shape and it loves me because I adorn it with all the clothes it loves to wear.

It did take me some time to get my head around being able to wear figure hugging clothing. To me it felt very, "look at me, look at me." Now I understand that it's ok as its best for my shape, of course also along with other styles. One of my all-time faves is the fit and flare dress. Now let's get into it and find out what we should and shouldn't be wearing if we are an Hourglass body shape.

Dressing the hourglass body

No you can't – lower deck

- Avoid low-rise pants, since these may make your hips look wider and your legs look shorter. Mid-rise and high-rise cuts elongate the leg.

- Skinny leg jeans should also be avoided.

- Square box shape hanging dresses, or anything else that hides your waist. Baggy clothes will completely hide your figure not to mention make you look wide. You have a fabulous waist and shape so let's see it.

- Pants and skirts that have too much detail going on. No chunky stuff, embellishments, and pleats. Anything that will draw the eye to your hips making them look bigger.

Yes you can – lower deck

- A pencil skirt is made for an Hourglass. The way it holds itself around your curves is perfect to show off your feminine shape, you have the body to carry it off. Wear it with a fitted top to show off your tiny waist and maintain balance.

- Flared and skater style skirts look great on your curves.

- Stick with mid-rise or high-rise pants, these cuts elongate the leg. Styles with wide waistbands and yokes are especially flattering.

- Boot-cut styles. The slight flare keeps the bottom portion of your leg in balance with your wide hips. This also creates a longer, slimmer appearance for your legs.

- Fitted dresses that elongate the waist, choose an open neckline to open up your chest and minimize your bust. From there look for a dress that fits your shape, nipping in at the waist at a lower point. Fit and flare style works with your shape whilst making your waist look longer and consequently the whole shape taller and slimmer.

No you can't – upper deck

- Avoid straight and boxy style jackets as they do not show your waist and will make you appear heavier.

- Baggy sleeves

- Flouncy blouses

- Anything lose fitting and with no shape is to be avoided.

- High necklines are a big no. A polo neck will make your boobs look disproportionately large. We want balance.
- No ruffles, pleats or chunky stuff going on up there. It will just draw attention there.
- No double breasted jackets and coats, all that does is add bulk.

Yes you can – upper deck

- Go for jackets that follow your body line and draw in toward the waist. Short jackets that stop just above your hips accentuate your curves in a flattering way and makes you look taller and slimmer. Look for form-fitting and belted jackets. Also, single buttoned jackets as they don't add bulk.
- Cardigans/tops with plunging necks, V-necklines, scoops, and sweethearts are a must. Wrap style works well too.
- Look for tops that will accentuate your waist and maintain the balanced look of your figure:
- Belted tops
- Tops with banding or nipping at the waist
- Form-fitting tops
- Tops that finish just below the hip line, this makes you look taller and slimmer
- Wrap-style tops.
- Tailored shirts and jackets.
- Fitted dresses that nip in at the waist showing it off. Wrap and fit and flare styles are fabulous.

Shoes

- Do not wear chunky shoes.
- A slimmer to medium heel works well.
- Wear a heel that's in keeping with your frame. Look for rounded toes or peep toes. Avoid pointy shoes.

There you have it. The key facts for the body shapes. By now you will have a good idea of what body shape you are. What you should be shopping for, what you need to throw out of your closet and most importantly what new and fabulous styles you can adorn your body with.

Remember no matter what size you are, every single shape has parts that we need to be aware of, has parts that we may love less then others but they are ours. Have our name on it and made for us, to be cherished by us. The red cherry on the very top though, is knowing how and what, so that cherry can shine like no other!

Oh… some bad news though. There is a high chance that you may need to go shopping. What a shame! This time I promise you, it will be effortless and fun, as you will know exactly what to head for on the racks. No more taking a huge armful of clothes into the dressing room and next to nothing looking right, coming out flat as a pancake. From now on you will be woop whooping from the changing room. Don't forget to make your notes in that super cute little notebook and keep it in your bag. Most importantly have fun, buy it, wear it and totally own it!

Could have
Should have
Would have

Emma – continued

I'll never forget the day I met Emma in the cloakroom at my kid's school. She reached out to a stranger, another woman, and mother to help her. I didn't know of course at the time, about her awful experience that had happened at the school with her girls. I helped her but she, in turn, helped me.

As her painful moment, pushed her to make a change about herself, it also pushed me to make a change about myself. She had no idea what she had done for me that day… of my realization of what I was meant to do with my life.

The ironic thing is, a few weeks later when the other mothers had obviously seen this new and wonderful change in Emma, their attitude towards me slowly started to change. No more snide remarks and comments as I walked past, no giggles and snickers with each other. Actually, thinking about that right now, doesn't their behavior remind you so much of those girls, who made nasty comments to Ella about her mum that day? Hmmm… our kids don't miss a beat, do they? Just take it all in like a sponge. Thirsty, eager little minds watching and copying. We sure do have a lot of responsibility, for those of us that are parents don't we?

Emma rung me up one day not long after, very amused, to tell me that a couple of the mother's from school had approached her. They wanted her to ask me, on their behalf, if I would consider having coffee with them. Ha-ha funny how things change huh. Just always stay true to yourself, don't change yourself for anybody. If I had taken on board all their laughs and negative comments… trying to bring me down, they could have really knocked my confidence. Made me actually second guess what I was doing, and what I was making to wear. To the point of giving it up, because maybe I was just a dreamer. It happens.

When it comes to your passion, you must have thick skin, do not take on board the negative, and carry on doing what rocks your boat. Be you. Now I have learnt that when you do tend to get a push back in some shape or form, often you are on the right track.

Unfortunately, there are people out there who can't handle other people succeeding – being fearless in going after what they want. Why? Because it makes them feel inferior, even if they could just as easily do it themselves. It is easier for them to keep in with people in the same boat as them, then their own life is not in question. Surround yourself with like minded people, this is so important. Those are the people that will support you, encourage you, and enjoy the process with you. Because they just get where you are at.

On a side note – I have learnt that in life, especially growing up with three older sisters and a big family, with all the different personalities, and the dynamics that go with it, relationships are a two-way thing. This is the time where it is NOT all about you. There are people in life who will take, and you will find they will be around while things are lasting and working for them. I finally came to the realization that when you are not met halfway, or not met at all for that matter, you need to stop, take a step back and understand, whether family or not, they won't always feel the way you do. That, when you do ease off that accelerator, not being the one to reach out and keep the relationship alive, there is often a deafening silence. Then all becomes clear.

When I finally got that, after many years, it was a most liberating feeling. Basically, it's ok, if you don't have this amazing relationship that you envisioned you should have. Don't beat yourself up. I love just being ME now and people who love me for me, are the ones that are already by my side. They totally have your back without a word said.

Back to the phone call with Emma. So I met with the other mothers, including Emma of course, and we ended up having a great time – with a few fun girl makeover sessions that followed. More designs were created and new friendships were made.

The Pear – The Emma

It's always all about finding balance between your top and your bottom.

To get a full and detailed list of what to wear and what not to wear, and all the types of styles and clothing you should be wearing, go to the chapter *When to say yes – When to say no – When to say never ever.*

So with Emma's outfit, she wore that day, it didn't help her in anyway whatsoever. Why was it so wrong for her?

Her tight leggings were pale colored so our eyes are drawn straight downstairs

They were super tight, not wider leg to give any balance. Instead, grabbing her everywhere, showing and highlighting everything, the full length of her legs.

There was the focus right on the thigh area with large flower detailed chunky pockets. Just making the area look even bulkier than it was, and again our eyes were sitting exactly where we shouldn't be looking – the thighs!

Now the top;

- It was baggy so it gave no shape at all, no silhouette of her waist, or her lovely slim upper body. There was no fitted shape upstairs, no showing off up there to stop us from running back downstairs.

- It was plain, boring, with no detail, so no visual interest.
- It finished right at the top of her thigh area… at her most problematic area. The thighs.
- It was a pale color, no bright or bold, to excite and stimulate us, so back down we go.
- It had a high neck, not showing any skin expanse or width, which is what we need to see, skin to draw us up and balance the body out.

So you can probably see now, why, when Emma looked in the mirror that day after the comments about her looking like an elephant, and that she couldn't fit her pants properly. With her own eyes, when she stood in front of the mirror, it was then she could truly see for herself.

This made her feel low and unattractive. The vision she gave out, did nothing to show off her best assets, it only emphasized her problematic parts. Which we all have, whatever shape we are, there are aspects of each one that we need to watch out for and learn how to work with it, to our advantage.

Once you know your shape, like Emma now does, it will be easy for you, as you will know your Yes, your No, and your Never clothes!

Now what SHOULD Emma have been wearing? Here are some options

Tops

A bright colored or bold print top with lots of visual interest and detail. With a V, square, deep, round or sweetheart style neckline. One that shows some skin width up there.

A fitted cut to show off her slender upper body to give off a stunning silhouette. Go for it! Have fun, get creative, you are lucky because out of all the shapes, yours and the Apple can go crazy upstairs.

Bottoms

Skirts – an A-line shape that has the flare and width toward the bottom. It does a brilliant job of balancing out the upper body and deceiving the eye at the thigh area. In a dark color, keep it simple and classy with no detail or interest. Preferably a longer length and not above the knee. So what do we want to do? Think… oh, that is so boring down there, let's go up! Hooray for going upstairs.

Pants – a pair of pants we want to see a straight or even better, a wider cut leg. If you don't like wide leg pants, just at least go for a little width at the bottom. Just no skinnies and nothing tight. It just makes your thigh / hip area appear bigger than it is. Give it balance. Keep the front flat, no extras added.

Dresses – one that emphasizes the waist and upper body. With an A-line, flare skirt or a wrap style dress. Again longer length. A fabulous bold print and pattern or vibrant color with detail on the top. Remember you can get fussy and flirty and fun. Again with a gorgeous neckline that shows some skin to bring us up top. Just think – skin. You have many options to choose from. Lucky you.

Accessories – complete the look with some small wedge shoes for great balance to your frame. For a bag, go for a short shoulder bag that finishes and sits above or on your waist, no lower. We don't want anything sitting around the thigh area.

So this is what Emma SHOULD have been wearing. There were so many things she COULD have been wearing, and she WOULD have, if she had just known her own body shape.

She conquered

Emma with her new styles was feeling fabulous. She could not remember the last time she felt so good about herself, inside and out. It had definitely been many years. She even had more friends now as she was feeling more confident in herself to speak to other people. She and John now have monthly "date nights" which they just love. It is their special time together, they get a babysitter, and off they go. They had made a list of all the different things they would like to do and go to. Put them all into a hat, and each month they have a turn to draw one out. Whatever is on the paper is what they do for the date night.

And with the girls too, she has more energy to give. She is not sure how that worked, but overall, she just feels better about things… happier. The girls also enjoy going shopping with her now, and pick out things in her colors, now looking for tops and dresses with her correct necklines. They had a fun time. They were also happy to see their mum happy. At school, she had always wanted to get on the school committee. So she did, and looks forward to deciding which outfit she is going to wear to each meeting. Often the other ladies comment, saying how lovely she looks. How things have changed, yes, things are different on the outside now, but also the inside. Because she was feeling better within herself it just seemed to have spread to other areas of her life, without trying.

She has started walking everyday as well. Something she had been meaning to do for ages, she had always loved to walk. She decided it was a small thing to do for herself every day, so she makes the time, no matter what. She has even started a little shoe fund; she loves her shoes, and with now knowing which to choose, it is her secret little pleasure. John certainly appreciated the new looks each date night.

Every fortnight the group of mothers that have now become good friends, all meet for a coffee/play date. They have some great times talking kids, husbands and outfits. When Emma now walks into the school, she walks with her head held high, her shoulders back, even with a little sashay to her walk. Go Emma. You rock!

Mandy – continued

Mandy is one of Emma's friends. Both their eldest kids were in the same class together at school and are great mates.

Now let's take a look at the Apple shape.

The Apple – The Mandy

The Apple is best described as round. In other words, your waist is not defined and is your widest part. But you have a great bust, so make the most of it and focus upstairs not downstairs. That is your tactic. You need to get your tummy in proportion and lessen the impact on the rest of your frame. A clear definition is what you need between your breasts and your tummy.

But let's recap; you may remember what Mandy wore that dreaded night. A white super tight, high necked short tube style dress. As you read below you will see why that outfit wasn't loving her body. It didn't highlight any of her great parts.

It was super tight, grabbing every bump and bulge that was available to be seen. There was no definition of any area, certainly no definition between; the above waist to above the bust line. There was no focus, drawing us up top away from the problematic area. As her tummy was the widest part of her body, all we could see was this and every part of it. Shapewear underneath would definitely have helped, but again with it being so tight and white, there still would have been some issues to deal with.

It was white, which as a block color, especially makes everything look brighter and bigger. Tending to give off a marshmallow effect. White shows everything when super tight – the rolls, the dimples, the works, it is terribly unforgiving. Even the best bodies in the world still have to be careful with tight white. There was no bright color or pattern to confuse the eye, no darker color at the bottom with a brighter color or print at the top to draw us up there. Just tight white everywhere.

It had a high neck, which covered all of her chest area up top where we really needed to show. An expanse of skin was needed up top to bring the eye there and add balance to the lower half. Not only did it cover her whole chest but her neck as well.

It was shorter in length, sitting above the knee, this is not a good length for the Apple. You want the length to be on or below the knee. Again this was just bringing everything up to condense it into one area, whilst making her look shorter and wider.

The shoes were stiletto, petite style shoes, which highlighted the contrast of the upper body to the slimness of the legs. It didn't balance out, making the top half look even heavier.

It was plain fabric with no visual interest. We need to draw up and deceive the eye, as this is the key. There were no patterns/prints at the top, or anywhere for that matter. There was nowhere to go but back to the middle. The eye was not confused at all.

And, she had a bag that was large and sat right on the tummy area.

You can see how wearing the wrong thing on your body can do so much damage to the outer appearance. It is not hard to wear the right thing and avoid this, you just need to know how and what. So when the daughter and mother at the work event, called Mandy out on being pregnant, you can see how the image of the widest part being the tummy gave that unfortunate visual.

What should Mandy have been wearing? Let's check out some options.

Tops

A perfect top for Mandy would be a deep V-neckline, sweetheart or square, something showing skin. A vibrant color print or floral with some visual interest on the neckline or on the shoulders. The short sleeves could have a soft ruffle, they would be finishing above the bust line or go for the cap sleeves. We don't want the sleeves hemline sitting around the waist area. The length of the top finishing just under the hip line. This will bring us down over the tummy area.

Bottoms

Skirts – for this shape the A-line skirt in a darker color to complement the floral or print above would be great. I would choose the darkest color in the print/floral and aim for that. Or you could just go for black. The skirt needs to finish just under the knee and with the soft flare to balance the frame out. The skirt needs to be plain and simple and no fuss, as it will all be happening upstairs. You could also go for a print skirt, and simply make sure there it's lots of visual interest going on in the top. All you need to think with this shape, and that of the Pear, is UPSTAIRS.

Accessories – complete the look with a wedge shoe, which not only is comfortable but nicely balances you out. If you are adding a bag, choose a clutch or a longer shoulder bag as you don't want one finishing and sitting right on the waist area. It just adds bulk.

Pants – if you want to pick the pants option to go with the top, choose a pair that is either straight or slightly flared. Knee or under knee for summer length. Zip at the side and no fuss or detail. Plain and simple is the way to go.

Dresses – a gorgeous cut A-line dress would look fabulous on Mandy. A sweetheart or square neckline with buttons in the middle that are bold and pretty that take your eyes right in the middle at the top of the bust. Whammo! Or some detail and embellishment on that neckline. As you know I am partial to buttons so think they would do the trick perfectly. The dress would gently flare out so there is still great shape but not tight, and not hanging square. The length would finish just a smidge under the knee, I think this is a super elegant length.

I would choose cap sleeves to just grace the top of the arm area. The fabric would be in a bold print or floral. Complete with wedge shoes.

Mandy, you are out of the starting blocks girl.

So this is what Mandy SHOULD have been wearing to the party. There were so many things she COULD have been wearing and she WOULD have, if she had just known her own body shape.

She Conquered

Mandy really struggled after that awful night of fleeing the party, in tears and mortification. She felt very low for a few days after. Then got to the point she had to snap out of it and do something about it. It was not good for the boys see her like that, nor fun for Simon either. She was the only one that could help herself. Simon had been worried about her. So it was time to give herself the "suck it up princess speech".

The first step was chucking out all the clothes that were anything like those that she wore that night. There is no doubt, she knows for sure now, that isn't something she should be wearing. Out goes the super tight anything, out goes the short stuff, out goes the white… out goes this… out goes that! Out, out, out!

What a wonderfully liberating feeling and what a great new start. As the old saying goes, out with the old and in with the new. It was time to find out what she should be wearing for her body shape. It was also time for a new haircut. She had been wanting one for a long time but just had no inspiration for herself and too busy for what she would call "nonsense" for herself.

Not anymore, she is going to pamper herself. She rung up, right then and there, and booked herself in to the salon the following day. Next, she booked herself in for a manicure – why not! Maybe, just maybe as painfully and awfully dreadful as that experience was, there had been some good in it after all? I mean she never would have made this change for herself if that hadn't happened. It had driven her to get brutally confrontational with herself.

Next was her wardrobe, yip she needed a new one, as she had almost thrown out everything that was in there. She texted her friend Emma who she hadn't seen in a little while but had kept in contact with. As mentioned, their kids used to go to school together but when she and Simon moved out of the area, not too long ago the kids changed schools too. Their eldest kids used to be in the same class. She had seen the change in Emma just before they moved. She was looking fab, and they did have similar body shapes. She knew Emma would help her shop for the right clothes.

After an amazing new haircut, and beautifully manicured nails, she met Emma for lunch a couple of days later. Emma just loved her new look. She would have been overwhelmed if Emma hadn't been with her to shop. She helped show her what type of clothes to pick out. Mandy got a whole new wardrobe and fell in love with one of the outfits so much she wore it home. She doesn't remember being this excited about getting dressed in forever. Emma had turned up with a little present for her, she had unwrapped it while they were having lunch. It was the cutest little notebook ever, bright pink, with white polka dots all over. It was jammed full of notes on all the styles, etc. that she now must shop for, so she will never buy the wrong thing again.

Bless her. She was feeling so great, new clothes, new haircut, and new nails. It feels so good to just do something for myself, she thought.

The following month they were invited to a friend's birthday party, a short time ago she would have cringed at the invite and made an excuse to Simon why they couldn't go. Not anymore. She chose one of her fav outfits and off they went, having the best night in a long, long time. She had so many comments on her new look, and she could tell Simon was super proud of her. Guess what? Mandy is also now sporting something on a certain finger on her left hand… you got it, a gorgeous pear shaped diamond that sparkles just like her! You did it Mandy. You sucked it up and not like a princess but like a queen!

Jayne – continued

Jayne is the younger sister of Mandy's sister in-law Kimberley. Every now and then they will get together for family weekends at Mandy's brother Michael's holiday home. Most times they will bring Jayne along to have a break from her studies and have some family time and see her nephew Reece. Now, let's talk about the Strawberry shape.

The Strawberry - The Jayne

Jayne's body shape is the Strawberry/Inverted Triangle/Lollipop.

The shape has a generous bust, wider shoulders, long legs, and slim waist and hips (yes, hello!), which are the defining features of this shape. The key is balancing the figure and de-emphasizing the upper half, so there is no top heavy look.

Let's talk more about what Jayne was wearing that day at work when she read the awful email, and why she got those comments about her image at the office. It isn't hard at all to make this shape look great but this is what she was wearing;

A super tight top with a high scooped neckline to the very top of her collar bone that had ruffled cap sleeves, the top was also tucked into the pants below. Immediately this gave off a "shelf" effect which is not a flattering look. Meaning basically, that the boobs look even bigger than they are, and look like they are sitting over the waist, being the shelf. There was no definition there. The ruffled sleeves drew us up to the top again, and the shoulders, that are already a little wider so we don't want the focus there. It is all looking very top heavy. Then the fabric is not only super tight but it is bold with thick red and white horizontal stripes, which make everything look wider and bigger on the top half of this shape.

A high waisted fitted skirt that finished in length, with the above top tucked into it. It is black and simple and plain with no visual interest at all. So what do we do? We go back upstairs to look some more. All the tight long fitted skirt does is emphasize the slim lower half making the top half look even larger and out of proportion. Don't get me wrong, it is great the bottom half looks slim but not when you are not appreciating it and just going up. It's all about the balance to make that gorgeous waist pop and show off the rest of the body.

The shoes she wore were plain wedges with wide straps that crossed over. These looked heavy on her slender legs. Slim stiletto heels look gorgeous on your legs and look in perfect proportion. Go bold and have fun with your shoes.

The bag she had to go with her outfit was a handbag that she wore as a shoulder bag, which of course sat right under her armpit sitting right on her boobs level. It was in a fabulous bright red, which is gorgeous, but not with this outfit and not on Jayne. This just brought more attention to this area.

For the accessories, she had on a bright gold and black chunky statement necklace that sat above her boobs over the top. Again all eyes back up in that central area.

What should Jayne have been wearing? Let's check out some options

Tops

A fabulous v-neckline or a square or sweetheart/big scoop, showing some skin would be great. Fitted at the waist finishing on the hip bone. In a darker color, but you could add a pop of color with a waist belt to emphasizes that gorgeous waist and draw the eyes there. This style top gives balance and eliminates that too heavy top look. You could also go for a peplum top if you are wearing a more fitted fluted style skirt. Peplums are fab for bringing in the waist and giving an illusion of hips. Again, pop a belt at the waist, with a fun color or print.

Bottoms

Skirts – an A-line skirt would be a great option as with the gentle flare at the bottom, it adds that balance that we need for the upper body. Wear a gorgeous bold color or a print and create your own personal style. You could also go for a more fitted style skirt but fluted or tulip, again giving the same effect to balance the frame.

Pants – go for a mid to low rise and a cut that has more of a bootleg or slight flare. Remember, we need to do what we did with the skirts and add a little width at the bottom to balance out. You can get creative with the pants and choose ones with cool pockets, zippers or details on the hips at the front and pockets at the back. Add visual interest. Choose a fab print or bold color, and if you are going for a three quarter length for warmer days, again, just that slight flare at the hemline. You will look taller and your curves will look fabulicious.

Dresses – you look super gorgeous in a fit and flare style, go for a scooped neckline with fitted a bodice that nips in that waist. Then the full skirt will swish out giving off a fabulous balance and flair to the rest of the body. If you need another layer, add a little blazer with a button at the waist, as this always works well and is classy. Have fun and you can always add extra definition to the waist with that belt.

Accessories – choose a fab stiletto slim heel shoe to show off those slender legs. Add a shoulder bag that finishes at the waist or a clutch. Use a belt to bring us back to that small waist. Color? Patterned, gold or silver. There are so many cool belt options.

So this is what Jayne SHOULD have been wearing to work that day. There were so many things she COULD have been wearing and she WOULD have, if she had just known her own body shape.

She conquered

Jayne had really hit a turning point after her unfortunate email at work that day several months earlier. Since then, she had buried herself in her studies even more than normal. Eric, that guy in her building that sent the email to Jayne, and not his friend had changed her life, woken her up to herself. When Jayne saw him in the mornings in passing, she just pretended nothing had happened, and when he murmured hello said her normal cheery hello back. One thing he would have noticed is that she no longer wears what she used to wear. So he might not be that excited seeing her everyday now. She found out what she should be wearing for her type of body shape. All those old things have gone, and now she actually gets many comments, good comments, with what she wears.

It took her a little while to get used to her new way of dressing as it was different to what she had dressed liked before. She was actually thankful that she had found out, as she would have gone on for years not knowing any different. It is was quite fun getting dressed and picking out her new looks now. She really does see the difference for herself in her appearance, and feels good to have learnt that – just because you absolutely love something, like her old tops, it doesn't mean you can or should wear them.

Last month she had also met the loveliest guy, he was at her law school and very different to any others she had met. She had sworn after the last couple she had gone out with, no more relationships and would focus on her career. David was different though, they had started seeing each other out of work/study, and loving their time spent together.

The biggest thing is that he is not clingy or unable to handle what she does, as he is also juggling the same type of work and study load as her. He is always telling her how beautifully she dresses.

Now, she will take a day at a time, but with her new style and old confidence, life is feeling pretty good.

Jayne you are going to be the best dressed lawyer in town. High-five!

Georgie – continued

Georgie met Mandy through her husband Nathan, as he is the soccer coach at the sports club where Mandy's eldest son plays. She met Mandy one day when she was there helping out with the morning tea. They have got to know each other quite well but don't really see each other outside the club days. They both get on well. Let's take a look at Georgie's shape.

The Pillar – The Georgie

Georgie's body shape is the Pillar/Rectangle/Column.

This shape is generally taller and the shoulders, waist, and hips are similar sizes, and they have lovely long legs. So they need to show off their slender legs and arms.

They don't have broad shoulders but their bust is the same width as their slender hips. They don't have much in the way of a waist, tummy or bottom. The shape is very much straight up and down, the only curves really being the bust.

The key to making Pillars look their best is to introduce shape, and emphasize curves. We will get into more detail about the shape later.

That night Georgie was out shopping at the supermarket, someone mistook her for being a man, which really shook her up. What she was wearing was doing nothing for her at all, it was hiding her shape and not bringing out any part of her womanly beauty. Let's see why it wasn't working for her, this is what she was wearing that night.

A square shapeless top with long straight sleeves that hung heavily from the shoulders and bagged her out. There was no shape, no cutting into the waist, nothing, simply just a box. It was grey and was a longer style jacket finishing well below the hips. With the body shape already being straight up and down, all this did was emphasize that fact.

The pants were plain and also grey like the jacket, so now we have one big long block of color. They were also straight cut pants, showing no shape, just the straight line of the legs. As the jacket was longer you only saw some of them so it made the torso look out of balance and unnaturally long.

Shoes were a very thick chunky heel and a long shoulder bag. The bag had a long strap that added more "long". The chunky heels needed to not be so chunky, a medium size balanced heel would have worked well.

What should Georgie have been wearing? Let's look at some fab options

Tops

A scooped neckline is great as it softens the squareness, or a V-neckline works well too. Wear a top with a gather, nipped, or belted waist. We need to bring the eyes to that waist to create curves. A top that is lovely and fitted and finished on the hip bone is fab. Break up the torso and wear a fun bright bold color or print. Angular shapes are cool and work well. You can wear any length sleeve but the wider the better, this will add a little shape and take away from the straight up and down look.

If cooler weather, layer with a little jacket with a button at the waist to complete the look. Layering is a great way to break up the body.

Bottoms

High waisted look amazing on your frame, just don't wear a dropped waist. Add interest to the hip area with pockets or zips and pleats. Add a belt around that waist and make it pop. A slight flare is what you need to wear, showing off those long legs. Capri style looks fab on you too. Again, go for color or print.

Skirts – high waisted are gorgeous on you as they show off your lean frame but still bringing our eyes to the waist. Pop a belt there too. A-line cut will flare out gently from the waist creating an illusion of hips and shape. Add some visual interest with pockets or embellishments on the hips. Go for color or pattern.

Dresses – either a gathered/pleated waist extending into an A-line skirt is super. Or go for a fitted dress with a great tailored cut, just don't wear one block color. Angular dresses are great as they chop it all up.

Accessories – big, bold and beautiful is what you want to do here, have fun and get creative with your own style. Accessories of this type for you, create a statement look. You can wear many different shoes and they look gorgeous on you but keep total balance, so don't wear too chunky a heels, and don't wear too thin a heel. Keep it in the middle for perfect balance for your frame. Add a belt and nip it in to accentuate that fab waist – let's make some curves. When adding a bag you can pretty much choose but remember are trying to create curves. I would suggest a bag finishes at the waist area to accentuate the waist and break up the body.

So that is what Georgie SHOULD have been wearing that day

There were so many things she COULD have been wearing and she WOULD have, if she had just known her own body shape.

She conquered

Georgie got home that night after the incident at the supermarket and threw out everything from her closet she could get her hands on that looked anything like what she was wearing. Leaving a huge pile of clothes in her room. From that moment on, she felt like a new person. She was determined to look after herself and put the effort in – never to be accused of looking like a man ever again.

That following weekend after pretty much eliminating her whole closet, she decided it was time to call up her friends for a girl's day out. Shopping, dressing up, dolling up, the works. They had attempted before but her heart just wasn't in it then, she had no interest in herself. But now she was ready.

After a fabulous fun day with her girlfriends and a new wardrobe later, along with new makeup, and new foils in her hair (to lighten it a little), she was exhausted but felt AMAZING. She caught Nathan staring at her so many times it made her giggle. Everyone at work could see the change in her even though she had her uniform on, there was just something different about Georgie now. It wasn't just the super blonde highlights in her pixie haircut that made her green eyes pop even more. Her smile was bigger than normal and she had a little sparkle in her eyes that wasn't there before.

A month later she and Nathan decided it was time for a very well overdue holiday. They booked in some leave and did it before they would change their minds. They had a wonderful time and Georgie had all eyes on her dressed-in her new looks that made her body look so beautiful and womanly.

You put yourself first Georgie and you are a stunner! You totally rock.

Alice – continued

Alice is the daughter of one of the doctor's at Georgie's hospital. She works close to the hospital so after she has picked her son up from school, she sometimes pops in to see her Dad. She had said hello to Georgie several times in passing, but now know each other. Now let's see what the Hourglass shape is about.

The hourglass – The Alice

Alice has the hourglass shape, as we best know it.

This shape is all about those womanly curves. The bust and hips are well balanced and there is a beautifully defined waist (yes Mandy, I know).

The upper body is proportionate in length to the legs, which are shapely. The waist is small in comparison to the hips and bust.

The key is to proportionally dress the top and bottom, while accentuating the waist.

That day in the office bathroom is one that Alice will never forget. The hurtful words of those girls really made her question herself and get honest with the reflection staring back at her in the mirror. What was she wearing that day? What made her look like this "football player" they had talked of?

A bulky, boxy looking straight cut jacket with double breasted gold buttons. It had a high scooped neckline and a stand-up short collar. It was a beige color and finished in length just below her hips. It was not only baggy, with no shape at all, but it made her look wide and hid her waist, like she had none at all. The buttons gold and shiny drew attention there and added to the bulkiest look of it.

A full flared dropped waist skirt with pleats, that also had fake front pocket flaps that sat just under the pleats. All this did was add fuss, heaviness and basically enlarge the whole area. The dropped waist made her look, not only wider than she was, but also shorter, it hid her gorgeous waist once again. The look was big and baggy with no shape whatsoever. Married with the jacket above, you can now see the entire look she was giving off and the skirt was all beige in color.

Wedge shoes with a thick ankle strap, more heaviness and the wide strap at the ankle just cut her off at the ankles, making her look shorter. Her bag she had worn with her outfit that day was a short shoulder bag, and yes finishing and sitting around the bust area and above the waist.

You can see after going through her outfit that this definitely wasn't loving her body the way it should. Her best part, her waist, was non-existent, and the outfit had only added width and shortness to her womanly frame hidden underneath it all.

So this is what Alice SHOULD have been wearing to work that day. There were so many things she COULD have been wearing and she WOULD have, if she had just known her own body shape.

Let's look at her options and see how she could have changed her appearance to highlight her great attributes.

Tops

A beautiful fitted V-top that nips in at the waist, scooped or sweetheart open neckline. Something that doesn't cover up your chest area or you look top heavy and out of proportion. We need to minimize the bust area. Peplum and wrap style tops work well. No fuss up there, keep it simple and focus on your waist. Belted tops are super cute with a pop of color right on your most fabulous part. If you need that extra layer, add a crop jacket that finishes and sits just above the hip line giving you perfect balance and proportion and accentuating those curves. A single button do up is absolutely the way to go.

Bottoms

Skirts – skater style skirts are great on you as they nip in at the waist then fall outwards. The fitted pencil skirt was just made for your curves.

Pants – pants that have mid to high rise and a wide yoke is especially flattering as it elongates your legs. A slight flare/bootleg style keeping them clean and simple is the way to go.

Dresses – fit and flare are so great for your shape. Fitted bodice with a big scooped, V or sweetheart neckline. I am a little partial to the sweetheart as it has that classy girly look to it. A wrap crossover bodice is also a winner. Then the full skater skirt style flares out to swish around the knee line. This look elongates your waist, making you taller and slimmer. Add a cute belt to bring it all together and flaunt that little waist.

Accessories – shoes with a thin to medium heel. No chunky shoes. A peep toe or rounded toe work really well, just not pointed. Belts are your thing, make them pop with pattern and color. When adding a bag choose a clutch or a short shoulder bag that finishes at the waist.

She conquered

Alice had a wake-up call that day. It not only made her have a hard think about herself and how she was actually feeling, it was owning up and being truthful to herself. Was how she was looking, make her happy? Did she feel good? The girls had also made comments about her partner James too, that made her think that she wanted him to be proud of her and how she looked. It wasn't just for herself. Deep down she knew she could do better, she had got too comfortable and lazy with herself. She was the only one that could make a change though. Her, and only her.

So she did, she made some changes.

She got some help and she attacked her closet like a crazy lady. She had decided there was no mucking around, if she was going to do this, she would do it. She also rung up her old gym that she had stopped going to, her old personal trainer was still there, so she booked him in for next week.

The following month it all came together. New clothes, new look, she felt like she had a new relationship with James too and the beginnings of a fitter stronger body. Alice also realized she could still have a more corporate business look, for work, without having to wear a boxed up bulky looking beige suit. Now the girls at the office are the ones asking HER where she got her clothes from. How things have shifted for the better.

The following quote from Zig Ziglar says it well.
There are people who will do you wrong, thank them for making you strong.

Alice thanks the ladies for turning her life around. Alice, you did it, you made it happen and look at you now. Smoking it!

How do these five fabulous ladies shop now?

EASY is how they shop. They all keep their little notebooks with them in case they ever forget what they are meant to be looking for. They all know the styles and cuts that match their shape and only try on those things. They can happily take an armload of clothes into the change rooms now and only put them back on the rack, if they can't afford to get them that day or they preferred a print or color over another.

And so, if you were a fly on the wall, you would only hear, 'Yes, yes!' coming from the changing room, you will only see happy women stepping out and going up to the counter. NO MORE depressing shopping trips, walking away feeling awful about themselves. No dreading having to go shopping when they get asked to an event and don't know what to wear. They have also learnt their own colors, so on top of the styles they have that extra boost and glow with the outfits as well. Lastly, they all have the best fitting bras to give that extra wow. Not to mention some fab shapewear for backup for that super sassy little number for the perfect silhouette. All the ladies now totally enjoy looking for new clothes. The ladies that all once despised shopping now love it. They have all admitted that they go out more socially now with their friends and feel they have a new found confidence. They now own it. Just the way it should be. I love happy women. Go the sisterhood. You make my heart happy.

My Fashion Emergency LBB

You now get to see my top secret double loaded little black bag!

A practical chapter this one but with a twist.

OH DEAR... you are going to get to know me just a little bit more. I think it's time to top up the wine glass or have that second hot chocolate... don't forget the marshmallows. I must quietly confess I have had many of these. Not wine and chocolate, well yes that too, but I am talking about the fashion emergencies. Not that one should be proud of this, but I must say it has given me plenty of conversation starters over the years. Or actually, I should say, more truthfully, lots of getting laughed at during these conversations. I do tend to be a bit of a klutz. But rest assured, the advice I'm giving in this chapter is good advice. I admit I go a million miles an hour, always have and always will. It's the way I love it. I am either zilch or 1000% with whatever I do. So I think the clumsiness comes more into play here, as I always seem to be juggling too many balls in the air. Don't get me wrong I absolutely love juggling (not literally, I couldn't do that to save myself) but as I am doing what I love every day, there is always something new and exciting happening.

During these fashion emergency moments, when I am normally in a state of humiliation and mortification, I have always wished that I had been better prepared, so after all the mishaps I have come up with a list of things. I feel they pretty much cover one's plights. So instead of my little black dress, we call it – my little black bag. No one really knows what's in it, what secrets it holds but soon you will. It's what I would call a women's peace of mind, a double loaded backup pistol... no that sounds wrong, but you know what I mean. Anyway, I digress.

When I was making a list of the things I wanted to include in this book I felt that this wee chapter was an absolute must. Maybe there were other clumsies out there like me? Not only will it give you an insight into my clumsiness, and some giggles, it will also give you ammunition to use in different situations – that may or may not arise in your life. That is what having backup is all about... right, it is there if you should ever need it.

First step

Choosing your FELBB (fashion emergency little black bag), you can go for the option of just a bigger bag that has a large secret compartment with a zipper. I say with a zipper for a reason. The first time I got all my FE items together I just slipped them all into a large side compartment in my bag. One day when I accidentally dropped my bag (as one does) some of the things rolled out... I realized this, in itself needed to be noted. It was just another embarrassing moment to deal with. As those around me were trying not to look too closely at the odd things that continued to roll out on the floor, heading their way, for all to see. So you see what I mean? I even managed to have a fashion emergency (FE) moment with my LBB.

Now back to the larger bag option. Listen to me when I say, go for a zipped compartment! Mine, of course, has a gorgeous gold and bling zipper. Any chance whatsoever to add either of those things and I am in. Just a little bit posh should we say. Make sure you put a little something extra on yours too. I mean why not?

The second option is to get a decent sized zipped toilet/cosmetic bag and just pop it inside whatever larger bag you are carrying. It stays in there and never comes out… until you need to unleash it, which hopefully is not often. If you normally carry a small handbag you may need to invest in a bigger one, if you want to be part of the club and have the full FE items. Oh no. A new bag (what a shame). So sorry to have to suggest a little shopping trip. Can I come? So now we have established why we need the LBB and what type of bag it should be.

It's time to now attack the list. This is like one of those times when you see someone giving a speech, they are holding a small bit of paper, then all of a sudden they let it drop and it is about ten miles long. Yip. Those. It's one of those.

But first, let me say that all of these items on the list can be bought in mini and travel sizes. So do not be freaking out right now when you see this list. You are not going to need to get a gigantic, big, ugly duffle bag instead!

My LBB top secret list, for women who want to have that double loaded backup, peace of mind kind of feeling goes like this:

Nipple stickers, chicken fillet, wipes, deodorant wipes, plasters, cotton buds, makeup remover squabs, safety pins, doubled sided tape, mini sewing kit, pluckers, pads, tampons, mini stick perfume, pocket size pantyhose, G-string, tube top, tissues, mouth freshener spray or peppermints, butterfly earrings, superglue, floss, rescue remedy, stain remover stick, heel caps, lint roller, feet spray, static spray, bug repellent, garment deodorant remover, foot heel cushion, thin scarf, nail file nail kit, bra clip, hair tie, rubber bands, bobby pins, brush/comb, mini hairspray, sanitizer, set lashes (if wear falsies) and non slip shoe base grippers.

I see you, you are bolt upright now on your elbows saying out loud, 'Shut uppp' right now but read on girlfriend, settle back down it will all come together in the end.

Now we have our list, and for my own, very real (unfortunate) fashion emergencies. You will understand after reading a few of these dilemmas, why there are certain things on the above list. So relax and get ready for a giggle or two at my expense. You're welcome.

My first day at work

It was my first day of work, officially in the corporate world. Main street in the city, high rise, one of the top floors (for NZ) super flash, everyone was very much in suit and tie kind of dress. Me… well I had a fitted pencil skirt to just under the knee, a bright little blouse, waist belt, cropped blazer and of course my stilettos, completed with my gold jewelry. My heels are one of my favorite things in life, I won't go anywhere without heels. I adore them.

After parking in our car park, which was not far from the office, I headed down the main street. Waiting at the crossing, the buzzer went and the little man turned green to cross. I walked across. It was busy so I moved over to the very far side of the crossing and off the zebra a little. Just before I stepped up onto the curb, I went to move forward and got yanked back suddenly. What?! I looked down… my heel had got stuck in the grate. Note to self, that is why you stay on the crossing area. Are you kidding me? I looked up and the little man was now blinking red. I was actually on the road now just off the crossing itself just in front of the curb. I was pulling with my leg to get the heel out, trying to not look too obvious. It's all good people, all is well, not much to look at here. The lights turned green for the traffic. I tried to hide my panic. I looked up at the cars directly in front of me and spot two men in the car pointing and laughing. OH the humiliation. There was no way I was leaving my favorite pair of shoes in that gutter grate! That was all I cared about.

I pulled my foot out, got down and tried to pull my heel out of the gutter. There I was squatting with one shoe on. The cars can just go around me I don't care. After about a minute, which felt like a day, I very gently managed to wedge my precious shoe out! Horaaaay! It was a little worse for wear, the heel was scraped and a little wonky, and the heel cap was gone, but still wearable. So I jam it on my foot, stand up, quickly stepping off the roadside and onto the curb. If a little awkwardly. With no heel cap I was feeling a tad off balance. I then hear some clapping? Looking over, there is a group of people that had obviously been watching my dilemma with great delight. I smiled with a nervous embarrassing giggle and a little wave, and rapidly walked into my new building. The doors were directly opposite the crossing.

At the bottom of the building was a café, which I then realized all the people in the café had probably seen the little theatre production, right in front of the window. The majority of them would also work in the building. Yippee for me. You go girl. I had not even got into the building before something had happened. Sheesh (this is where I would eye roll). I mean really?

I hop into the lift with what feels like too many people, I am not so great in small places but all is fine if it is brief. We stopped at a few floors on the way before mine at the top.

On one of the stops before, a lady stepped out, she turns around and says to me, 'keep an eye on that heel huh, very impressive the way you got that out' and smiles, then is gone. More people than I thought had obviously seen me at the crossing. Hope you enjoyed the production people, next showing time – never.

The doors open at my floor and I step out, open up the large glass double doors leading into my office. First day! I am still feeling slightly ruffled but I made it. After being introduced to everyone, I pop my bag down at my desk and head out to make a coffee. It looked simple enough, I turn the machine on, noises happen. I click black coffee, put my cup under and wait. Loud noises, then a gurgled choke and silence. Ummm… I press a few more buttons… I mean seriously how hard can it be… what is wrong with the stupid thing? I so need a coffee right now. I lean down to look closer, all of a sudden it goes on and spurts out coffee, half in the cup and a side squirt on the front of my super cute blouse. Well, that was a misfire if ever I've seen one. Something is seriously wrong with that machine. Yip. Ok. One heel down, and now one blouse. Next minute one of the admin girls come in, I don't think she could believe how making a coffee could be so hard. I look at her and laugh, 'Ha ha having a bit of a blonde moment.'

She looks at me a little blankly. I always use that in a weird situation, it just seems to cover it all. It also just seems to come out of my mouth before I have had time to even think about it. She makes me a lovely strong coffee, very quickly and effortlessly I might add. I go into the toilets and with soap from the dispenser and water, try to clean my blouse up. Not much good, the dark brown mark still sits proudly right in the middle, if not now smeared even bigger. I am just going to have to do my blazer up, um yeah… nuh, a bit tricky, as it doesn't really do up over my bust. It's more of an open look kind of blazer on me. Oh well, I'm sure by the time I get back out there the others will know I almost broke the coffee machine, and made a mess of myself. I only have lunchtime to worry about, facing the public in my messy shirt. The blazer will just need to be suctioned in and hope it stays done up.

Ahh, coffee… wonderful, I pick it up from the bench and walk down the other end of the office to my new desk. Putting my coffee down very carefully and sit…. well I went to sit but as I did, my chair scooted out from under me, because of course, it had wheels didn't it. I was so careful putting my coffee down, I didn't look properly where I was parking myself! Yip and out she goes, the chair and my butt and I hit the floor. Is it actually humanly possible for all these things to happen to one person in the space of an hour?

Oh, the pain in my back, I'm meant to be taking care of my back. I am not even meant to be wearing heels yet after my accident but there was no way I was wearing flats to work. Not a chance, there is no power in flats. Not that I am feeling incredibly powerful right now. I carefully and painfully get up. The girl across from me says, 'I cannot believe you just did that, we are going to love having you around. Welcome on board.' Everyone laughs and claps in the office, oh well I guess that broke the ice… and nearly my back again, my tush too for that matter. It was very fragile after my accident from years ago. Not my tush, well that a little too but my back. Oh and it was it was so sore.

I swapped chairs after that, as that one wasn't cutting it for my back and I needed hard, upright and no dumb wheels. After organizing my desk and finishing my coffee, starting to relax after my full on first hour. I decided I would start making some client calls. So I pick up my pen and pad and headed into one of the private rooms by the front of the office, shut the door and start to call.

I was talking to one of my clients and then I hear a loud shrieking noise, then I see people from the office running past the clear cubicle I was in. Well, it was an office but the top half was glass, so really all I could see was these heads running past. Ahhhhh, what's going on? My client is still talking to me, all of a sudden my door is pushed open and my boss puts his head in the door saying, 'quick hang up and get out, the fire alarm is going and it's not a drill, there is apparently a fire.' Then he is gone.

I hear my client calling out on phone, 'Christina, Christina are you ok? What's happening, what's that noise?' I say to him, 'sorry… fire, gotta go.' As I put the phone down I hear him call out 'what?! Christina?!'

No time to grab my bag, the office is already empty, I head out the front doors to the lifts. My boss and some of my colleagues are waiting at the top of the stairs at the fire exit. I hear someone yell out from inside the staircase, 'make your way down now'. We have to walk down the stairs to the lobby. Oh my goodness, my back I can't do this! With my heels on too, and I don't have my bag with me, that has my back pain relief either. I take my shoes off amongst weird stares. Too freaking bad. We were on the top floors of the building so you can only imagine how many flights of stairs we have to walk.

By the time we stepped out into the lobby I felt dead and in pain. I just wanted to sit in the lobby but of course everyone had to go outside onto the street to wait.

After about half an hour we get the all clear to go back into the building. There had been a small fire on one of the lower floors and was now under control. The drama had ended, well for now. There were lines of people waiting to get into the lifts and everyone seemed to be packing themselves in like sardines, all in a rush to get back to their desks, I mean my poor client, I had just hung up on him.

Next lift opens and we all pile in, and pile in, and I'm thinking, ahhh people, I think there is a lift limit! My boss and a couple from our office were in there, the rest from other floors. I count eleven people in this lift. I start to feel the apprehension climbing, I am trying not to focus on how squashed I am and how many people are in here. Oh why did I count them?

I look at my boss and he looks red and sweaty, and whispers to me, 'I am not good in small spaces and I just want to get out of here.' Well, that makes two of us mate! I'm not so great in here either I say to myself. We stop at the first floor and just two people get out. Doors close and up we go then a jolt and stop.

There is complete silence for a moment, then a guy says, 'Don't worry it will just be for a mo.' I can feel my boss start to squirm beside me, I sneak a look at him and he is in one serious sweat. Oh dear, then the lift starts up again, everyone breathes a sigh of relief… Oops too soon! Another jolt and it stops and this time after couple minutes nothing. A guy presses the emergency button, a voice comes on and he tells the lady on the other end what's happened. She said, 'Yes, we are having a few issues, we will get this fixed ASAP. Is anyone in there pregnant or have any heart problems?'

Ummm, issues? And exactly what type of issues would those be?! What good was it for them to know if someone was about to give birth to a baby or have a heart attack? I mean like they could have done anything anyway.

Oh wonderful, this whole day had just got to be a dream, not a dream, maybe a nightmare. I mean what are the chances of this actually happening after everything else this morning?! The voice carries on talking to the guy.

My boss says to me quietly, 'I need to get out of here and now.' Well, we are really bonding now, aren't we? To distract him and myself, I just start talking about the job and other stuff, pretty much just rambling rubbish. At this point feeling a little panicky, there are just too many people in this lift… it is over loaded. We cannot be in here for long. Calm down girl I tell myself, pull up ya big girl panties and keep control of yourself.

All of a sudden we all almost fall onto each other, well if there had been room to fall onto each other, and the lift after a big jolt takes off! Hooray! Relieved smiles all around and cheers. The next stop quite a few get off, then one more and then it's our floor. When those doors open my boss literally runs out in front of everybody. Ok. I may start drinking tonight. I feel like I have just run a marathon, well walked one anyway with a massive amount of flights of stairs, and the stress of being stuck in a lift. I just want to go home. I don't like today anymore, can I order a new one… please. Thank you.

After that, thank goodness, the rest of the afternoon goes smoothly, I ring back my client who had been literally left hanging after the words, 'fire, gotta go!' He was very pleased to hear all was well. I popped downstairs to the café to quickly get some lunch. In my super tight about to fly open blazer and have my lunch back up at the office, which had amazing views of all over the city and the harbor. That was a lovely peaceful moment.

So that was my first day. Now as you can imagine, later I had wished I had some things to help me combat all my dilemmas during that day. This is where my LBB would have come to the rescue.

If my little bag had been with me what would I have used out of it?

- Heel cap for my broken stiletto
- Superglue to glue on my heel cap
- Heel pads to help the pain in my feet from all the walking
- Stain remover stick or wipes for my blouse
- Rescue remedy to keep me calm through all the disasters of the day

The Wedge

You will be thinking I have a problem with shoes or heels as here we go again. The funny thing is on the day this happened I actually took a photo of it to show my friends!

This is a short story but interesting none the less. I had an appointment booked and had just arrived at the location. Cafés were "my office" most of the time. So I put my foot out of the car to get out, stood up and almost fell over. I look down and to my horror, the wedge of my shoe had come off and was sitting there on the concrete. I'm talking a big wedge as I wear super high heels. I could not believe my eyes, like only the very top part of my shoe and strap was there, with no heel at all. Zilch nothing. Right ok, so I was at my appointment, the client was inside and here I was outside my car holding half a shoe.

Think girl, think! There is only a pair of hubby's jandals (kiwi for flip flops) in the car and that's not going to happen. Options are, I take the other shoe off and go in bare feet, oh please no. The second option is I somehow try and put the wedge back on? Well, how am I going to do that? Stupid option. Last

I told you, proof of the troublesome wedge.

option, just bail, ring, and cancel. I cannot be hobbling in there with one shoe to a top client, I also cannot go in there with bare feet. There is no way I will be going in there in hubby's massive surfy looking jandals either. Should I really cancel though just because I only have one shoe? Oh my, why do these things happen to me? The client is already there, has taken time out of her day to meet me, with I imagine, an even busier schedule than mine. I can't do it, I cannot bail. I look into the café and I see there is an empty booth right by the front entrance. Ok, so what about if I just put the top half of my shoe on, and of course the other, and just pretend the wedge is there and like tip toe kind of. Listen to yourself girl… really? I mean unless someone actually looks at that shoe they shouldn't notice, right? Best plan, only plan. As the empty table is right by the door. I can quickly scoot straight into the booth then text my client and tell her I am sitting waiting at the table by the door. Yes!

So believe it or not, off I go with a very skinny top of my shoe with nothing under it and try and walk quickly as if I have a good old solid wedge there, and as normal as possible, across the parking lot and open the doors to the cafe. Who only knows who was watching? I slide into the booth so fast I whack both my knees under the table and cry out. Oops… a couple turn around in a booth in front of me and stare. I politely smile back, nothing to see here folks. All good. Cringing with the pain of my bony knees having just hit the wood, I text my client. A couple of minutes later she walks around from the other side of the cafe. I get out of my seat, standing up the best I could to shake her hand. All while staying firmly behind the booth. She must have wondered why I didn't just get out like a normal person. Oh lady, if only you knew.

After the meeting I told her I was staying on a little longer to get some work done before another meeting. After she left, I took both shoes off and fled to the car. I was over it by then. Sitting safely back inside my car I let out a huge sigh. Ok, I did it, but what a mission. Just another day in my life. How did I survive my childhood and all that horse riding?

Definitely another LBB moment. Now, maybe you are thinking, well yes, that would be a little black bag moment but who on earth has disasters like you? Yes, I do understand where you are coming from but you never know what type of situation you may end up in one day. Or even a friend, or some random stranger and you are able to help her because you are going to whip out your cute little black bag with a pop of bling and offer an array of weird and wonderful things to assist her with. She will love you for it. If you never ever have a mishap in your life (possibly, maybe, unlikely?) you can always help out another clumsy sister in need.

Now with this emergency, what would I have used out of my LBB?

- Superglue - to try and stick the wedge back on, at least long enough to be able to get through my client meeting.

- Rubber band / hair tie – to strap it around onto my foot. Not ideal I agree, but at least it would keep it on long enough.

OR you know what? Maybe I will start a LCB – little car bag. If I had an extra pair of heels in the car I could have just put those puppies on and that would have been the end of my problem! Slight problem – you don't always have your car right by you. Let's just say we should do that anyway. Ok, so one of the above would have at least got me into the café.

The Bikini and the Fillet

On the subject of helping other sisters out with your LBB, I did just that one day to my bestie. Yes, for once it wasn't me! We were at the beach, there was a game of volleyball near us. We had been sunbathing and hanging out nearby, and were asked if we wanted to join the game. We were in, so we left our bags and stuff on our towels, as they were close enough to where the game was being played. I had little shorts and a singlet on and my friend still had her bikini on. She had always had a real problem finding the perfect bikini she loved that also had a really decent amount of padding.

After a while of never finding what she wanted, she decided she would just pop some "chicken fillets" in. For those of you who don't know, they are squishy gel pads that you pop inside your bra top, to give you more cleavage and basically more oomph. They stick to your skin. They are meant to anyway. She had her fillets in her bikini, but as we were playing she jumped up and did an awesome pump on the ball. Wow, what a great hit, I was impressed but then as her feet hit the ground I saw this pinkie colored thing go flying up. Umm, what was that? OH NO, one of her chicken fillets had flown out of her bikini top. It landed on the other side of the net directly in front of a guy's feet with a slap on the sand. I quickly looked at him. He hadn't seen it, yet. I leaped forward and took off under the net with lightning speed, grabbed the fillet, running a few steps away and throwing it into a nearby bin and said, 'Oh people leave all sorts on the beach don't they?'

I walked back under the net and called out, 'We will catch the next game, we are going to get a drink'. My friend, meanwhile is just standing there clutching at her bikini top, looking at me like what just happened. Ha ha, and oh no, I had just thrown her fillet out into the filthy bin. But wait, of course in my tote bag I had my LBB and inside that was an emergency fillet. Out it comes and into her bikini it goes. No more volleyball for us but plenty of sunbathing and walking around. My friend is happy, she had a nice full bikini top again. So you see, it's not always me with disasters. The little black bag is for the sisterhood too.

This is my last dilemma I am going to share with you, well there are more. But you can't hear them all.

Passion, Fashion & Heart

A splitting day

I had chosen one of my favorite dresses to wear to work this day, it was an oldie but a goodie. It was a gorgeous dark teal, fitted style with a belt at the waist and little pleated neckline and cap sleeves. It also had a split going up the middle at the front. I had paired my new Gucci heels with it. It looked fab. I had a very busy day and was ending it with dinner with clients. I had come up in the lift after my first meeting of the day, opened up the double doors and walked into the front reception foyer. It was an open plan layout with gorgeous glossy floors, floor to ceiling windows all around, and reception in front. All the desks were to the left as you walked in.

I took a few steps in, then I felt a foot go out from under me, then the other, it would have won bloopers and surely gone viral if it had been on video. I felt like I was in slow motion just flailing, arms out trying to balance myself, like baby giraffes. I was literally skidding from one foot to the other, my bag flew off my shoulder, I dropped my case, it all just went to custard on the spot. Thank goodness for years of horse riding for balance, there we go, I've got this. Then suddenly a loud RIP, by now I was so close to the reception desk, so I reached out grabbed the edge of it to stop and steady myself. Phew. I look at the floor to see my stuff everywhere, then something catches my eye. I look down, Ahhhhh my dress is almost in half at the front! I have split the front split and it is seriously sitting up around my hips. I quickly grab my case from the ground and shove it in front of my ruined dress. I turn to the left.

Yip… there they all were, they had seen it and were in complete fits of laughter. Loud uncontrollable laughter. Meanwhile, as I was just rooted to the spot I suddenly remember I have a client turning up in…. I look at my watch… in about twenty-five minutes for an appointment here at the office.

What am I going to do? It is actually not possible to do anything in this dress, it is so far up. I can't meet anyone in this. I see my blazer hanging on the back of my chair. I go over and grab it and for now tie it back the front around my hips. What a sight to see. So at least now I am covered but I will actually need to go home and get changed, as I have meetings for the rest of the afternoon and then dinner with clients.

One of my colleagues takes over my meeting for me. After saying goodbye to them, they are still giggling away. I have one of the office girls oversized coats on that I have borrowed. Of course it is the wrong size and so long on me as well. I put my sunglasses on and head downstairs to walk up to the parking lot. I looked like I was about to rob a bank.

So that was just another disaster. The floor hadn't just been polished or anything. It must have been my brand new heels that were so magnificently new and slippery.

Now, had I had my LBB on me, what would I have used?

- A spare emergency pair of non-slips - to put on the bottom of my heels.

- My needle and thread emergency sewing kit - to sew up my split. It wouldn't have taken long and it would have at least got me through the rest of my day.

So there we have it. I think I have confirmed that every girl should have a LBB in some shape or form with them at all times. You may not be a klutz like me, but your friend or some other sister on the street could be. We have all got to stick together right. It's all about the sisterhood.

Now lastly I apologize for that little shopping trip you now need to take, for a new bag and for all your goodies to put in it. Have fun!

Perfect Color
Make it Pop Shine and Glow

How to look even more gorgeous than you already are – by matching your tones to your colors.

I am so excited to share this wonderful info with you on your tones and colours. It really does make a difference, and people will ask you.. what did you do to your skin? What makeup do you wear? How do you get that extra healthy gorgeous glow? Have you been on holiday? It's our little secret...it's all about you wearing the right colours for your tones..as simple and easy as that! Lots of people choose to wear and buy clothes according to the latest fashion trends and styles. This is usually aligned with the seasons. Instead, they should be picking out clothes in colors, based on their skin's natural tones. That is if you really want that ultimate look that will take you from great to absolutely fabulous. That's ok though, as many are not thinking about their skin tone when out shopping for their next closet addition. Unless you know about all your colors and tones. It's not something you are even aware of when shopping.

But now you do know. It is like learning what styles you should be wearing for your particular body shape. It really does matter and makes a big difference as you will get that extra pop and glow. It will also help you to choose not only your best colors but also jewelry, foundation, blush, eye shadows, lipstick and hair color.

Some colors can make you look like you have just been to a spa retreat for a week. Others make you look like you need to go for a month. So wearing the wrong color really isn't doing you any favors. It can make your skin look like you need a shot of vitamin D, or you can look like one whole blob of blended color.

Choosing clothing that will complement and enhance your skin tone is not hard. In saying that though, you do need some basic knowledge of color theory (which I give you below), and the ability to determine your skin's undertones.

Choosing the right shades of color for your glorious wardrobe will help you look fabulous, feel confident, and the super plus is that you will actually need very little make-up or accessories to look extra amazing. So what I ask, is not to love? Exactly.

The first step is understanding what skin tone and undertone category you are in. Our skin's surface tone is the color that you would describe yourself as having, e.g. (light, fair, medium, light tan, dark tan, etc.). Your skin's undertone is the color underneath the surface. You can have the same skin color as someone else, but a different undertone. When broken down, these are like this:

Cool (pink, red or bluish undertones)
Warm (yellow, peachy, golden undertones)
Neutral (a mix of warm and cool undertones)

Let me say though, there is quite a big misconception that pale girls can't be warm-toned. Yet many fair-skinned women have warm undertones, and dark-skinned women have cool tones.

Skin tone categories:

♠ Light
♠ Fair
♠ Medium
♠ Light/dark tan
♠ Dark tan/bronze

Tips on how to discover your tone

1. Blue or green veined babe?

Look at the veins on the inside of your wrist. Are they blue or green? If they look bluer, you likely have cool undertones. If the veins look greenish, you're warm. It's worth noting that for warm girl tones, your veins aren't actually green, they look it because you're seeing them through yellow-toned skin (yellow + blue = green).

If your veins are not very visible, find a spot on your body where you can easily see your veins. If they are blue, you have a cool skin undertone. If they're green, then you have a warm skin undertone.

Your notes

....
....
....
....
....

While a person's skin surface tone may change due to some environmental factors like the weather, your skin undertone or the skin tone that lies right beneath the surface tone will remain constant. Skin undertones are identified as the following:

Warm undertones – described to have peachy or golden yellow skin undertones.

Cool undertones – gravitate towards the bluish, red, and pink skin undertones.

2. Gold or silver babe?

Think about whether you look better in silver or gold jewelry (not which you like more, but which actually makes you look more radiant, glowing, and alive). Ask friends to help. Typically, girls with cool undertones look better in silver, white, gold and platinum metals, and warm-toned girls look better in gold, pewter, bronze and copper.

Your notes

....
....
....
....
....

3. The Neutrals

Think about what neutral shades flatter you the most. Do your skin, eyes and face look more vibrant and healthy in bright white and black hues, or ivory, off-whites, and brown/tan shades? The former means you're probably cool-toned, and the latter, warm.

Your notes

....
....
....
....
....

4. Eyes and hair

Your natural eye and hair colors can also help you to figure out your coloring. Customarily, cool people have eyes that are blue, gray, or green and have blond, brown, or black hair with blue, silver, violet and ash undertones.

Conversely, warm-toned women usually have brown, amber, or hazel eyes with strawberry blond, red, brown, or black hair. Their hair tends to have gold, red, orange, or yellow undertones.

Passion, Fashion & Heart

Your notes

....
....
....
....
....

5. What does the sun tell you?

When you're out in the sun, does your skin turn a golden-brown, or does it burn and turn pink first? If you fit into the former category, you're warm-toned, while cool tones tend to burn (fair-skinned cool girls will simply burn, while medium-skinned cool-toned girls will burn then tan).

Your notes

....
....
....
....
....

6. Are you a celebrity match?

Here are a few celebs who have cool undertones: Delta Goodrem, Scarlett Johansson, Megan Fox, Lucy Liu and Cameron Diaz.

Here are a few that have warm undertones: Halle Berry, Jessica Alba, Jennifer Aniston, Ariana Grande and Kendall Jenner.

7. What is the color that makes YOU shine?

There's no denying that certain colors will make you look more fabulous, regardless of your skin's undertone. Warm-toned girls should lean toward yellows, oranges, browns, yellow-greens, ivory's, and warm reds, while cool-toned girls should wear blues, greens, pinks, purples, blue-greens, magentas, and true "blue-based" reds.

Your notes

....
....
....
....
....

Are you a cool, warm or neutral girl?

Before you can choose your perfect clothing colors, you'll need to determine your skin tone. Skin tones vary from warm (yellow/green-based) to cool (pink/blue-based). Some people have a neutral skin tone that works well with both warm and cool tones.

Test using foundation

Be sure that you don't wear any makeup before doing this test.

Go to a department store and look for the makeup section.

Use the makeup tester to check your skin tone. Look for a shade of warm color, neutral color, or cool color. Apply a small dab of the foundation makeup to your wrist or on your face.

Choose the color that best complements your natural skin tone.

Test using metal. Be sure that you don't wear any jewelry or nail polish before doing this test.

On your left wrist or hand, try on a bracelet, wrist watch, or ring in gold material. On your other wrist or hand, wear a silver bracelet, wrist watch, or ring.

A white metal like silver will complement a person with cool skin tone, while the gold metal will look better on a person with a warm skin tone.

Test using paper

Before doing this test, again, be sure that you aren't wearing any nail polish or jewelry. Use a plain, white piece of paper and place your palm and hand on it. Turn over the paper to see your palms and arms.

Check if there is a distinctly blue or pink cast. If you see one of those colors, then your skin tone is cool. If you see an orange or yellow cast, then your skin tone is warm.

Test Using Comparison

Comparing your skin tone to others' skin tones could be helpful, they may also want to figure out their own as well. Ask some of your family and friends to stand in front of the mirror. Compare each complexion.

Skin tone looks pinker, compared with the others who may have cool skin tone. Next to the others, a person who looks more golden probably is inclined to be a warm color tone.

Test Using Yellow Fabric

Get a piece of yellow fabric, and place it beside your face. If you have a warm skin tone, then your complexion will be bright and glowing next to this type of color.

If you are a cool skin tone color, your complexion against this color of fabric will be the opposite. If you want to see a cool skin tone color that looks glowing, try to use a blue color fabric. You will notice that gives a good effect on the cool skin tone color and does the opposite for the warm skin tone color.

Test using white fabric

Another way you can determine your skin undertone is to get some white fabric around your neck and shoulders. If your face looks blue or pink you will most probably be cool skin tone.

If your face looks yellowish or peachy you will most probably have warm skin tone.

Neutral skinned people normally look greenish next to the white fabric.

Have fun and learn how to match your colors.

You can start mixing and matching colors together for you to wear. A fun way to do this is by using the color wheel. You may look at some colors and think – really? But yes go with it, as they will actually look fab together. That's because of this rainbow color wheel.

If you try to create an imaginary line to split the color wheel, half of the color wheel contain warm colors, and the other half are cool colors. There are two main ways to pick colors that will look great together:

Choose a gorgeous color from the wheel

Use your finger to trace the color opposite of that color on the wheel to get the color that will complement your first pick. The two colors that you got are called "complementary colors". If they complement one another on the wheel, they will also complement one another in your wardrobe.

Choose another color, look for the color on its left or right

These are what are called "analogous colors". Remember that half of the color wheel is warm and the other is cool, so you may need to play around with analogous color combos to find ones that match your skin tone.

Colors that make you look fab with any tone

White – can make any skin tone color look good. It does not require any certain color of skin, eyes, or hair.

Blush – can make any skin tone color look beautiful with a glow like no other.

Emerald Green – this happens to be one of my favorite colors. It looks stunning for both skin tone colors, whether you have warm or cool skin tones. For example, Catherine Zeta-Jones and Elizabeth Moss wear the same color, and both of them look gorgeous even though they have different tones.

Red – not only enhances both skin tone colors, it makes you feel confident and powerful.

Eggplant – not everyone likes this color, but eggplant doesn't offer any bad effects on any skin color. Instead it makes any skin tone look good.

Enhance your Complexion with awesome clothing choices!

Fair skin tones

If you have a pale skin tone, it can easily make you look washed out, with the wrong colors. Look healthy and vibrant and stick to a base of darker colors, such as navy blue, deep brown, black, charcoal, burgundy, and deep green. Avoid soft pastels, light beige and anything else too close to your skin tone, as well as bright colors, such as yellow or orange. Divine, rich, jewel tones combined with lighter hints of camel, slate gray or sand colors, can complement your skin tone rather than bleach it out.

Medium skin tones

Medium skin tones look the best with both light colors and dark or rich colors. Picking colors from opposite ends of the spectrum, such as white, light beige, stone grey, black and deeper jewel tones. Avoid wearing colors, such as light brown, mustard yellow or olive green. If you're on the darker side of medium, you can experiment with brighter, medium-toned colors.

Dark skin tones

Dark skin tones have the most options when choosing clothing, because looking washed out is not an issue. It's still important to be smart when choosing your colors. However, stick with a darker navy blue, black or charcoal as a base for your closet, but add in highlights of bright colors and those gorgeous jewel tones. Stay clear of dark brown, especially if it's similar to your skin tone. Pastel shades also look good on you.

Talk to me!

What skin tone will emerald green complement?

Emerald green will complement and enhance all types of skin colors from dark tone, earth tone to light toned people. It has an extra wow factor on people with an olive complexion, and fair-skinned people with both cool and warm tones.

What clothing color works with a warm skin tone?

The earthy colors of clothing works best for this skin tone. Pick out clothes in brown, red, and green colors. Grey, navy blue, and ivory are also great to complement this skin type.

What is the best fabric color for an olive complexion?

Having a color: grey for an olive complexion is lucky because… The best color for olive skin though is pink. It adds a glow to the person. Shades of the red and orange color group are also complimentary options.

What colors work best with dark skin tones?

The safest color for a dark skin tone is white, but if you want to wear any other colors, you can try shades of purple, pink, accents of soft to rich yellow, copper, gold and bronze.

Light colors compliment a darker complexion, such as peach, pale green, pink or orange. These colors will help to enhance a dark skin complexion.

What colors make blushed skin, brown eyes, and reddish brown hair pop?

If you have true auburn, red, or copper hair, you probably have yellowish, ivory, or golden undertones to your skin. If you have one of these hair colors, you might have green, hazel or brown eyes. For this kind of combo, natural and earth tones suit you best. Brown, dark and olive green, red, orange, gold, and beige look fab on you. Purple, navy, bright bold red, pink, gray and taupe will probably not do you any favours for your overall features.

Universal black will make your face look sunken and sallow. To wear black correctly, you should pair it with one of the colors mentioned above. Your face will glow if you wear a black dress with a jacket in one of the colors that compliment above.

How would a lovely jade color look on browner skin?

Brown skin is a perfect match with bright colors such as: yellow, peach, silver, coral, gold and other rich jewel tones. These colors look gorgeous on a brown skin tone. Jade is one of the jewel tones and looks great on the brown skin tone. Even so, it still depends on how deep your skin tone is.

What colors of fabric compliment silver?

Almost any color, anything can go with silver. If you want to achieve a frosted look, you can try white or blue. Mixing wine/maroon or purple with silver, will give you a regal look. If you're aiming for a more retro look, then try silver with orange or yellow.

How do you enhance a warm skin tone?

If you want to complement warm colored clothes, combine them with cool ones. For example, blue and green, pink and yellow, blue and yellow. The warm colors are highlighted when paired with cool colors.

Warm tones are attractive when combining with earth colors, as long as they're not too orange in color. If you mix warm tones with something that's more on the orange side, it would be a bit too much on the eye. Also, warm tones do not blend well with very dark shades, especially blue, because the dark colors will bleach out the warm ones. Lighter pastel colors will work better.

Is an orange color a good match for cooler tones?

Yes! Orange goes well with cool tones. You can team it with a dark color like black, which will make your skin tone look brighter and gives that extra glow we all love to have.

Cobalt blue is best for which complexion?

All complexions will work great with cobalt blue, as it is a lighter color and will show or pop better than any other darker color.

Phew… You have had a lot to take in, but like learning your body shape and the styles that you should wear, you just need to do the same with your color. Once you know your colors as well, you will have it all. You will be wearing the perfect styles and clothes for your body shape AND the perfect colors that will make you stand out and shine like a diamond.

Imagine going shopping with all that ammunition! Could be time for a color raid in your closet soon.

Your notes

....
....
....
....
....

What Lies Beneath......

Regardless of your size, shape wear can be the icing on that beautiful, rich triple decker, delicious decadent chocolate cake. Adorned with a gorgeous dark red shiny cherry. It smooths and tightens and enhances to reveal a fabulous silhouette. The right fitting bra and any shape wear is only going to give you that beautiful cherry sitting pert and pretty at the very top. So why not at least try it? Let's talk about… What lies beneath…

Firstly, let's kick off with the bra. Finding the right bra size can really be a mission for many women; it can be overwhelming and in the end, you just deal with it and wear what you have in the drawer. It is estimated that about eighty percent of women wear the wrong size bra. That's a lot of uncomfortable women out there, right? It is not a great thing for your ladies, nor is it healthy.

We need to look after these ladies and a bra that is too tight, is frankly my dear…not a good thing. We will learn together how to measure your bust and sort this out once and for all. Let's get you feeling comfortable and looking great with a perfect profile upstairs. We have enough going on in our busy lives, and we don't need to be wriggling, squirming, adjusting and pulling at ourselves, throughout the day. I mean, why the torture? Exactly.

We look after our skin, don't we? We cleanse and tone and moisturize, trying all sorts of creams and potions. Some of us go to spas, get massages, treatments, vitamins, the works. Yet giving our ladies the attention they deserve, to keep them well and healthy in their house, seems to just get thrown in the "too hard basket". Actually, once we do get it right, that's it, all done. When we know our correct bra size and type, then we know it, forever. It's not like our bra size changes every week or two and we need to keep getting a refit. They are far less work than any other part of our body. So this is really a one off effort and we have those ladies settled and comfortable. Do it once and do it right.

Discover your band size

A bra's band should fit snug, its cups should contain the breast tissue, the straps should assist the bra, not support the breasts.

90% of bra support is in the band. It's your suspension bridge, your foundation, your way to a perfect fit. The band is literally your bra's base and is built to support your breasts. If it's not secure, you're not secure. It should feel comfortably snug, and sit perfectly level around, front to back.

If it rides up your back, it's too big. If your straps are falling, it's too loose. It must be snug. A good rule of thumb is, if you can use two fingers to comfortably skim the inside of the band, it's correct. If there's slack in the back, your bra may be worn or you may need a smaller band.

Have someone measure around your chest with a tape measure, just under your breasts, and around the back. Make sure the tape measure rests flat on the skin and goes straight across your back.

The "old" advice has been to add five inches to this measurement – and then that is your band size (also called chest size). HOWEVER, adding only two to three inches (instead of 5) works better for most women. You can even try not adding to the measurement you get, and just using that as your band size. This is because the band is elasticated and because the bra band needs to fit snugly so it can provide about 80-90% of the support for the ladies – and then the straps (shoulders) only carry about 10-20% of the load. Oh dear, it really sounds a bit like a dump truck, doesn't it?

Finding your ladies perfect cup size

What's the gore?

The gore is the center panel of an underwire bra. The part of the bra that connects the cups in the front, between the breasts.

Not all bras have the same type or size gore, and some styles don't have this part at all. But if your bra has an underwire, then the gore will always be the part that's "center front" and it should typically lie flat against your body.

Your underwire should fit firmly against your chest without any gaping. Assuming your straps are properly adjusted, you'll know you've found the right band fit when you can lift your arms over your head without the underwire rising up.

The cup should hold your entire breast without the dreaded quadra-boob.

Have someone measure you. The measuring tape goes on top of the fullest part of your breasts. Record this number, and find the difference between that, and the band-size number. The difference tells you the correct cup size as follows.

While this is useful for determining the cup size, bear in mind that 34A cup does NOT have the same exact volume as 36A or 38A. Similarly, 30D does not have the same volume as 36D (30D is a much smaller cup than 36D). So, if you try on a 36B bra and the cup size fits but the band is too loose so that you decide to go to down in band size to 34, you may actually need 34C cup size so as to have about the same volume in the bra cup.

Even with a measurement, it is better to try on different bras and find out experimentally which one fits.

Just remember to go by the fit, not by the numbers. You have to try the bra on. If it fits right, that's your bra size, even if the tape measure told you differently.

To avoid breasts side walling instead of going straight forward... look for a bra with a four-part cup. The additional seam on the side, known as a "side sling", is great for helping guide your ladies forward.

What styles best flatter your ladies?

The shape of your breasts and torso are unique. Depending on your particular proportions, certain styles will look better on you than others.

Your bra will look better if it flatters the overall proportion of your torso. Ideally, your shoulders should look about the same width as your hips.

If your shoulders are broad, try to find bras with narrower straps, and a shape that plunges more in the middle.

If your shoulders are narrow, look for bras that create a more distinct horizontal line across your torso.

If your torso is short, a bra that plunges more in the middle can elongate your torso.

Think about the shape of your breasts. There are so many types of breast shapes and sizes.

How to tell if the ladies are sitting perfectly – are they where they should be?

If you are wearing an underwire bra, the wire that comes up between the breasts should lay flat (or as close as possible) to your breast bone. If you are wearing a bra with no underwire, you should have two separate breasts, not just "one big boob"… not a good look at all.

If the bra is a soft cup bra, you shouldn't have any extra, loose fabric. If the bra is a molded cup you shouldn't have any extra room in the cup. Your breast should completely fill the cup. If it is gapping and the band feels fine, then go down in the cup size.

You don't want to be spilling out of the cup – not from the top, bottom or sides. If the band feels fine then go up a cup size.

If you raise your arms up (do this a few times), the bra should stay against your body, not lifting up or off. If this happens, try a few things:

Adjust the shoulder straps by loosening them.

Pay attention to the band. Is it too tight? Or too loose? Or just right?

If the band is just right, and adjusting the shoulder straps didn't work, then go up a cup size.

If you have a more petite frame, and you find a bra that fits the band, and you don't quite fill the cup and you have already tried the next cup size down, and it's still not quite right – OR if you have the "right" size, the band fits and you fill the cup, but the wire is poking your underarms, then try a Demi bra.

A Demi style bra is different from a full coverage bra. The Demi has less wire by about an inch or more.

Try on different styles of bras. Every style fits and fills different and can "shape" your breast differently.

If your bra fits correctly, it should NOT be painful or uncomfortable to wear.

Extra tip: if a new bra has an adjustable back band with several hooks, it's best if it fits on the tightest hook. You'll have room to adjust it, when it stretches out, and all bras will eventually stretch due to normal washing and wear.

There you go, yes it is a bit to take in (pun intended). I do hope though, after reading all that, you will know how to find your bra size. That you are no longer freaked out or overwhelmed, or feel resigned to the fact that you will never be comfortable again, to lead a wriggle free life. Instead, that you have a new found confidence in looking for your ladies perfect house. That's pretty much what it is. There may be a little time involved but remember put the effort in now and you can forever hold your peace, or should I say they will be forever holding theirs. It will be like shopping for your body shape, now you know it.

Into the store you go, knowing what you need and what you want. It's now all about the fun of choosing what you love. There is such beautiful heavenly lingerie out there, it is waiting to be graced upon your body. When you know your bra size it's just about what fabric, colors, and patterns rock your boat. Then you shout, 'I want this bra, in this size, in every color.' Let's not forget that you will also now be comfortable throughout the day. Oh, the sheer bliss of it. No more writhing and wriggling. From now on, the tops and dresses you wear will look that much better because of what lies beneath. When you are walking down the street in your fabulous outfit and you have the most divine lingerie on underneath, you will feel amazing from head to toe… from inside out. You won't even realise that you are walking in a way, like you have a sparkling tiara on top of your pretty little head. Just the way you should. You got this girl! You have GOT this!

Enhancing your silhouette

Body shapers are wee-miracle performers. A fast and non-surgical way of looking great in what you are wearing. From super strong control styles that create wow factor change, to designs that reduce the appearance of cellulite. Shapewear has now become that piece in your wardrobe that is our little cherry on the top – a must. The trouble shooter for your problematic areas. Even though you are now dressing for your beautiful body shape, there will be an occasion when this will add that ultra wow look.

But there are a number of women who are not big fans when it comes to shapewear. They say that it's just so uncomfortable. I agree. Yes it can be if you don't have the right fit, BUT it's not on forever, and it is going to serve a specific purpose. Especially if your outfit is for an event or occasion and it matters what you look like. Us girls know that sometimes for beauty there is a little pain – right? When we just have to say to ourselves 'suck it up princess!' There are many different weights of shape wear too, you can get the light weight ones, which are way more comfortable to wear. Depending on what and how much you are trying to attack. There are so many options now with styles.

Many women say it's the secret to looking good, as it makes clothes sit where they should and just hang better. Giving you a really smooth outline and fabulous silhouette.

You don't have to worry about VPL (visible panty line) or "back fat" and the "awful muffin top". They steam roller over all the lumps and bumps. It is not really about making you look thinner, but it definitely helps. Lots of small sized women wear shape wear, even though many think it is just for bigger women. Thinner women can also be far from toned, with curves in the wrong places. They wear them because they say it just pulls things in. For a sharper more toned and "kept together" look.

There are different types of shape wear for different challenging areas.

We have:

The mid-section to create shaping, under bust to lift and support, compression to lift your tush and limit stomach and back bulge.

Cellulite control and also thermal weight loss support.

Let's look at them now.

1. For wow factor curve creation, the latex in this type of garment creates strong compression in your midsection. Many garments use different amounts of latex to create the shaping, the different weights as I just mentioned. So looking for this in the construction of shapewear is something to remember. It will reduce your midsection by one to three inches, immediately allowing you to look up to three sizes more tucked in and smoothed out. Which can, not only give an hourglass figure but greatly reduces any problematic areas. Wow. Worth a try.

2. The underbust shapers go right up to the area just below your bra. This type of shaper does more than just one thing. It supports the ladies, giving an instant lift and a fabulous push up effect. Yippee, with an end result of a leaner, elongated body look.

3. Shapewear is a great compressor and an easy way to get rid of that muffin top and extra bulges. But, while you are wearing a garment for these reasons, the one area you may not want to compress is the tush. Lots of shapers actually have built in designs that are meant to lift your tush, while reducing and eliminating back and tummy bumps and bulges. Sounds good right?

4. Now we have shapewear with built-in weight loss activity. Garments with thermal latex designs can increase thermal activity in the core. They increase the blood flow and move toxins. Studies have shown some sustained loss of inches with long-term results.

Cellulite Control

5. Some of the most effective non-surgical treatments for cellulite come in the form of garments you can wear. Anti-cellulite shapers use techniques like micro-massage with some using infused garments to smooth and create a more even toned skin. It reduces and eliminates the look of the dreaded orange peel look. Again smoothing bumps and bulges at the same time.

Now, with more knowledge of what lies beneath, in the way of shape wear and how it is important. It can make a massive difference to the outward look of that special dress or whatever it may be, for work and play. Imagine, you now know your perfect style of clothing, after learning your body shape and also how to obtain the correct bra. The perfect colors for your skin tone PLUS the kind of shape wear options, to help give you that wow factor with what you are wearing. Tighten, freshen, smooth, lift, enhance and elongate… worth a try my dear.… worth a try!

Oh no. I have just realized I have done it to you again. Made you go shopping that is. Sorry about that. No, I am not sorry actually, because at the very start of this book, I did tell you this was going to be all about YOU.

Fact File Shape n Style

We are going to talk layering. Wearing loose and tight, your tush, jean styles, and outfit ideas. So let's get started!

A loose fitting piece over a fitted piece can look gorgeous when paired with the right garment. This style is one of my all-time favorite looks. I always feel chic when I wear my fitted jeans and a classy white blouse with a bang of color (from the accessories). Of course, let's never forget the pumps, for that extra superlicious pop.

Styling tips

Go for thicker fabrics for fitted pieces and a flowy draping fabric, like rayon, silk or chiffon for the looser ones.

Change up your loose dress

Just because your dress is a little big, it doesn't mean you have to chuck it out. Find a cool patterned belt or one with bright colors, depending on the fabric of the dress. Pop a belt around your waist and pull out some of the material so it gently hangs over the belt. Or sit the waist down on the hip more and do the same if that suits your body shape better. If you have a shift style dress and just want to wear it a different way, do the same for a whole new vibe. But remember, that adding a belt must be right for your body shape, so check your notes.

Marry up loose tops with tight pants

If you want to wear an oversized top or sweater, wear leggings or skinny jeans. If you want to wear harem or leisure-style trousers, wear a tighter top/shirt or jacket.

A flowy draping blouse as mentioned, is always a pretty fabulous thing, especially when paired up again with skinny jeans or leggings. Don't wear a loose top or loose bottom as you will look like a sack has been dumped upon you. Yes, not a great visule.

My fav Lilika Luxe top and skinnies

Wear a super cute blazer over your relaxed fit dress

This will give you a whole new look. Full length or knee length. Any loose fabric around the waist gets nipped in when you button down a blazer, giving you a great silhouette and creates a waistline that flatters your shape. I personally love a one button blazer and prefer a slightly more cropped look. But remember to work with your rules for your body shape.

Blazers and crop jackets are always a great addition to many outfits for the cooler months, always giving a posh vibe for that top layer when you need it. This would have to be my go-to top layer.

Skinnies + loose tops – super cool, cute and chic

Skinnies are a very popular go-to cut, pairing them with flowy blouses and longer tunics for the perfect balance of shape and proportion. Look for the darker wash denim styles for a slimming silhouette. Or depending on your body shape, you could go for the lighter wash.

Loose fitted but with a great cut buttoned shirt, married with the right color of skinny jeans for your body type is another fab look.

For a cute and casual outfit, try a pretty, relaxed fit blouse with a pair of dress shorts for a sassy night look with strappy heels. Or keep it casual for day wear with a pair of denim or chino style shorts with sandals or pumps for a perfect easy to wear look. You can also pair this with a casual black skinny or distressed look jeans.

Another great option is tailored pants for the evening. I love the look of either a white blouse with a pop of color from the accessories, or go for a bright block shirt, or a pretty pattern with subtle accessories.

What I find so comfy and super cute, is a button down shirt with a crop top over the top with just the bottom and the collar poking out, along with the shirt cuffs. Paired with skinnies and pumps, it's cool, classy and a casual favorite of mine.

Jeggings. They look just like a pair of jeans, but are soft and stretchy when you want a legging feel

Loving this look in my Lilika shirt and crop top look.

but a jean look. These have been very popular. An oversized top and boots is another casual comfy look.

Your lace dress from the warmer months can also work for autumn/winter when you pop on a cute cardigan, tights and cool boots. This is a rather adorable girl next door look.

Pair a relaxed fit sweater over another relaxed fit top, add skinny jeans and a funky pair of ankle boots. If you have block color tops add a print scarf to bring it all together.

Wear cool high socks under high boots and over leggings, paired with a tank top and a short blazer. A casual adorable and slightly playful look. I tend to go for the tank tops with the scooped hem, which don't cut straight across sharply, and has a soft edge look to it. When paired with a cropped blazer that does go straight, it gives some visual layering interest.

Choosing loose linen trousers and pairing it with a fitted cropped top is an elegant look.

If you have a bigger style top, wear something short on the bottom. And if you're wearing something loose on the bottom, pair it with something that shows off your arms, chest, shoulders, or back. It gives balance. I love the look of a loose fitting top with a slightly wider neck so you can wear it as a slash neck or off one shoulder for a really sassy but chic look that shows a little bit of skin. Then wear it over a tight mini skirt or tailored shorts or leggings/jeans. Or do the opposite and wear looser on the bottom and something on top that shows a little skin, as just mentioned.

A tunic-length top in a bold block or statement print is another super comfy and stylish outfit for a lazy mood completed with either pumps or sandals depending where your day is taking you. I am a complete sucker for heels and totally in love with them. For me that outfit would be a no-brainer with the pumps, wherever I was going.

Maxi skirt + tee + jacket

Maxi skirts are great. You can get your fitted styles or your looser gathered look ones. Both styles look fab with your fav tee and a crop jacket for when you need that extra layer. Super cute.

In my favourite Lilika Maxi skirt look

Oversized sweater tunic

A cool tunic sweater will look awesome with leggings, jeggings, skinnies or tights. Boot socks sitting just above a pair of knee boots. Also cute with ankle boots. I find a funky ankle boot, whether it be a pattern or cool color, is something I always find myself wearing to give that extra push to an outfit. This tunic sweater look can be a lazy boho style but still a chic look.

Knit sweater

A knit loose fit sweater in a soft pastel – looks effortlessly stylish and pretty, matched with either jeggings or leggings in black or grey. I have always loved baby pink and grey. A scarf with some pattern and knee or cute ankle boots and you're good to go.

Layer me up and layer me right!

Layering is so versatile and fabulous and totally changes a look when done right. It is also great when moving from day to night and changing temperatures. Here are some tips.

Layering is versatile and practical and can also look chic all at the same time. You have to get it right though to carry the look off. It gives you a brand new look and style and also covers you for the changing.

Choose the right inner layers. Start with a basic, lightweight top (a solid neutral or striped may do)

Keep the under-layers more fitted to keep your slim shape.

Wear outer layers that can be easily added or removed.

Layer a cardigan, shirt or crop jacket over a fitted top

For a personal and stylish look, mix different fabrics – have fun and create your own personal style.

Using color

Think about your colors when layering, it is essential for creating a look that is cohesive and feels connected. You don't want to look like there should be a performing monkey on your shoulder.

Layer on the layers

Several layers of knits that work with your body shape is a warm and attractive way of layering, then add a fun color or patterned scarf.

Mix your textures

Don't be scared to play with texture and mix it up a little. It isn't a good look to have all of the same, especially with texture. Create visual interest. You learnt already with the body shape chapter where and where not to add the visual interest.

Leather looks

Leather is great because it is warm without being heavy and thick. There are some amazing quality faux leather around. If you go down that route, make sure it is a really good quality. It will then sit right and won't look cheap and ill fitting. It will add elegance.

Avoid multiple bold patterns that overlap

You can wear multiple patterns in one outfit, just remember to give them some space. So you are not wearing a colliding chaotic ensemble.

Pick your lengths

Same lengths are prone to look heavy and can also be unflattering. When layering always try and go for different lengths. For example; if I am wearing skinny jeans, shirt and a cropped jacket with pointed front, I will go for a straight across or scooped hem top or shirt that is longer than the jacket. I just love cropped jackets so I wear them often – even if just a little, I will normally have the under garment peeking out to some degree. Layering can also be flattering and slimming when done right.

Scarves are a great way to achieve a layered look. There are so many options and they give that extra sparkle to any outfit. Bold block colors, pretty or dominant patterns, and prints. They have a sophisticated look about them. I especially love them with a blazer. They just tie in and complete a look in a simple way. Taking a lazy outfit into one of chic interest.

Accessorize

It is always the detail and the finishing touches that complete a full look. Even just a gentle light accessory can make all the difference. I love gold so have my favorite chunky gold curb link bracelet and a plain gold bangle. I find between the two I can make them work for many outfits, and also married together.

I have never liked heaps of accessories so I tend to stick to simple pieces. If I need something with some "wow" I tend to go for a bright color rather than anything too fussy. This is just my own personal preference. It can be very different of course when I am dressing my models for the runway! I also wear bigger earrings and no necklace, or a necklace and no earrings. It is easy to go overboard with them and de-rail a look. Using accessories are so important though, just like the icing on the cake with a cherry on the top. It brings it all together. Just think about it as you go.

So there we have it, you now have some tips and ideas on layering and matching your loose and tight. Have fun and create your own style. It's what fashion is all about!

Your notes

....
....
....
....
....

Looking WOW in your jeans

Let's talk about jeans – our super comfy go-to pants, with so many styles and so many cuts. Which are best for you? Let's start with stretch.

Stretch jeans are made out of a type of denim cotton (or cotton/polyester blend) that incorporates a small percentage of elastane, a stretchy, synthetic fiber, also known as spandex, or lycra, into the fabric.

When shopping for either stretch or rigid jeans, you will know by now, you must look for a pair that works for your body shape as well as giving thought to the stretch factor.

Stretch jeans normally include about one to three percent elastane.

If you are between jean sizes, it's a good idea to buy stretch jeans in your smaller size, as they will most probably loosen up after a few wears. Remember, stretch jeans are meant to fit you snugly.

If you are not sure, try sitting down. You will know soon enough. If you can sit without getting cut in half, or feeling a degree of muffin top, you should be good in this size.

If you are a plus size, you may want to shop for a body contouring skinny jean. Most of the brands carry jeans for the curvaceous body.

How stretchy you want the jeans is totally up to you. The combinations below are assuming the stretch is combined with a high quality denim.

1% stretch – a great jean to contour your body, with just enough stretch to make you look fab while still being comfy. This is my personal preference.

2-3% stretch - once again a great contouring jean, at the same time even more comfortable. These you could wear anytime and anywhere.

4% stretch – this one is a super comfy and super figure hugging, for an all-around jean for work and play.

So you see, it is a personal choice. Go with how they feel and think where you would mainly wear them and what they would be for. I have different jeans depending on what I am doing and where I am going. I have rigid ones and a little stretch through to the maximum stretch. Skinnies and straight legged. That's me though, some people will happily have one pair of favorite jeans for everything. You will know when you put them on, it's either a yeah-nuh, or it's asking the sales girl to cut off the tag cause you are wearing those puppies out the door!

Your notes

....
....
....
....
....

Time to talk about your tush….

You know you want your butt to look fabulous…

When buying a pair of jeans, one of the first things you do when trying on a pair is to turn and check out your butt in the mirror. That's because you already know the right jeans can do magnificent things back there – the wrong ones can make it look… well pretty bad. Let's be straight up.

Even though jeans are a casual look, if you know how to wear them they can be classy and sexy. My all-time favorite look is a pair of skinny or straight cut jeans, soft draping shirt, a blazer if cooler, and a pair of vibrant or patterned pumps. Hello… in love right there!

The back pockets are pretty crucial and DO matter. They can significantly change how your butt looks in a pair of jeans. We all have wonderful shapes and wonderfuly shaped butts. Like the rest of our body shape though, we have to learn how to cover them in the right way to make them look as super-hot as can be.

Let's talk tush shapes. It's always a fun read with me huh? As you may already know there are contoured jeans you can get with the butt lifters and molders, etc. built in. If you want to know what and how to wear a standard pair of jeans, here you go.

Is there even a butt there – do you have a flat looking butt?

Pick flap pockets, don't do the rigid denim.

Steer clear of the boyfriend styles of jeans – their relaxed fit can make it look low and even flatter.

Try the styles with flap/bulkier pockets to add interest, detail, and volume.

Go for tighter-fitting styles to give you some shape and lift your tush up.

The lighter denim and the ones with the washes, pattern and prints will give some oomph to your tush. It deceives the eye. You may remember this from when we learnt our body shapes.

Are you bubbling out at the back?

Stay away from small back pockets, they will accentuate the seat area.

Don't let them high ride and don't let them go too low either. Medium rise.

They need to fit snugly but non-gaping at the waist

A contoured seam just above the back pocket should nicely hold in your curves.

Keep it simple, no interest and detail will work best.

Do you have a wider load at the back?

Do not wear wide-leg jeans. They just grab you at your widest part and that's about it.

The back pockets really need to be positioned close together, visually it will give you a thinner looking tush.

Keep them simple and go for jeans with basic, mid-size back pockets.

Don't choose flap pockets, bulk or detail. We don't want any visual interest back there.

Plain, plain and more plain.

Wear the darker washes, no light washes.

Does your butt hang low?

You must have pockets. If there are no pockets it will seem to hang even lower.

We want pockets that are positioned higher up, it draws the eyes upwards not down.

The bottom of the back pockets can't be lower than the bottom curve of your butt (where your cheeks meet your legs). If they are, you have turned into a pancake.

Don't go for the boyfriend style jeans; you want to look for tighter-fitting jeans. Your butt will look like it is on the ground. Not a good look.

Do you have a curvaceous butt?

If you want to slim down the look of those curves behind, don't add bulk or detail or interest. Keep simple and flat.

No flap pockets, they just add oomph.

Pockets that will enhance your butt and make it look best are larger, plainer back pockets that are quite wide and are positioned lower.

You really need to try and find jeans with pockets that start mid-way down your butt, and end at the tops of thighs.

Do you have a butt shaped a little like a triangle?

A triangle butt is basically when your widest part is where your hips meet up with your thighs.

You must get strategic with the position of the pockets. You want ones that are on a diagonal or sitting higher toward the waist, this will draw the eyes to the middle of your tush, not on the outside of your thighs.

So there you have it and now you know what will give you an amazing looking tush.

Let's talk jeans styles now

The skinny jeans

These are a popular jean as they flatter quite a few body shapes.

Super fitting and designed to accentuate your shape and follow those lines.

They are cut in from the hip to the ankle, giving you an elongated look and are super easy to style up or down. My personal favorite.

The boyfriend jeans

Designed to shadow menswear, boyfriend style jeans are one of the loosest and most relaxed cuts out of all the styles.

The relaxed fit and totally worn-in look, are super comfy and cool favorite.

These were originally inspired by women who liked to borrow their boyfriends' clothes, and have become a real favorite style.

They fit loose from the hip to the bottom and normally sit a little lower on the waist.

They are usually distressed and just plain washed.

The trouser jeans

These are pretty much the wider-leg jean with a tailored cut. Great and easy to style. They normally have a higher rise and are fitted through the hips and cut wider through the rest of the leg, with the widest point at the hem.

A great style jean for bigger thighs

They are comfortable to wear and flattering to the shape.

Trouser jeans have a classy look to them.

The straight cut jeans

These jeans are just as they sound and are cut straight from the hip to the hem.

I love this cut of jeans also, they are so versatile and can be worn with just about anything.

Having a simple, classy look to them, they are also comfortable to wear.

They are a great fit; tight but not too tight, loose but not too loose.

The straight cut pairs well with just about everything in your wardrobe.

The boot cut jeans

Boot-cut jeans normally have a lower-rise waist and are cut slim through the thigh, subtly flaring from the knee to the hem.

They are designed to fit around boots, hence the name.

These are our main jean styles, so hopefully you now have a little more knowledge around shopping for the jeans that suit your shape, so you can look and feel wow!

A Sprinkle of this and A Dash of that

*M*y favourite beauty items, my tips on travel, shopping and dressing from sunrise to sunset.

These are my fav beauty items that I simply adore and want to share with you.

Totally in love with my L'Oreal *Miss Manga Rock* mascara. When I don't have lashes for a certain trip or event this is what I wear every other day. I have had so many people ask me if they are fake, so this mascara is a super option if you are not a false lash girl but want the look. With my green eyes and olive complexion I always go for blackest black. I love really black lashes. This mascara thickens and curls something amazing. The L'Oreal black eyeliner fine tip is fab too.

Another L'Oreal product I love is the shimmer lip gloss. As I like a more natural look, I go for the nude or baby pink for that little pop of day time color. For night, I go a few shades deeper. I have always, always loved the gloss look above anything else.

For my skincare regime I have used for many years, the brand- Living Nature is gentle, natural, and never caused my sensitive skin any irritations. I use the cleanser, toner and day moisturiser. Then I use the Zeba Absolute Oil as a night oil before bed. You will read more about Zeba in a moment.

Zeba Absolute Oil is also a great product that can be used for all sorts of things. The key ingredients which I find fascinating are Myrrh & Frankincese Essential Oil. Myrrh & Frankincense date back to ancient times and have highly effective healing properties. So really quite an awesome oil. It has twenty eight uses to date and growing. It reduces the appearance of scars and stretch marks, while also improving skin-tone and firmness. It also works to reduce lines and wrinkles and helps to heal sun damaged skin, rashes, and eczema. As you can see, I love this brand- it's a winner. Best thing is, most oils leave your skin with a greasy feel. Not Zeba. You will one thing about me by now - I am all or nothing!

I also love the *Thin Lizzie* bronzer and have used this for years and love the minerals in it that seem to give that extra pop and glow. With the season shades, it is so easy to choose and you are ready to party. Plus their super soft big bronzer brush is divine. I do not believe that just because a product is the latest thing out that it is necessarily the best thing. As I have just mentioned I have used this bronzer for years and some would call it a little 'old' but I don't care. If it works and I love it, that my friend is all that matters.

For my foundation I adore the Fitcover brand, it is so light and has awesome coverage, it feels like you have no makeup on! It gives me a fresh glow with the perfect shades. I don't like the feeling of heavy makeup, so I'm in love with this. It is sweat resistant, so even when you are working out, active, just life on the go (hello!) your face stays looking fab and flawless!

I never used to apply foundation/concealer with a brush but now I do. For some reason I never did it, only ever used the sponge. Now I do, as can't compare the great and even coverage I get, especially around my eyes. My mother tends to get dark under her eyes, and I don't know if it is just a Greek thing or not, but she passed this onto me. So with using the little brush to get right under my eyes and corners of the eyes, it stays lovely and even.

For my hair I love the Zeba Absolute Oil *mentioned earlier*, when my hair is still quite damp I just put a tiny bit on my hands, rub them together and run it through the bottom half of my hair. In saying that I have also used it on my hair dry and it works well too. As my hair is pretty thick and wild, it gently tames it, defining the curl and gives amazing shine and softness. I can't keep myself from running my hands through my hair! Remember I don't have the nickname 'Bichon' from hubby for nothing.

So for my beauty stuff, that is pretty much me, as you can see I am quite simple when it comes to that. It doesn't mean that I don't try lots of new stuff I absolutely do! I just don't change products for the sake of changing products if what I am using I am already super happy with. When I find something that works and I like it, that is me, I am done and don't meddle around. All the above are products that work well for me, that I love the feel and look of. Most importantly, how they treat and look after my skin. And as you get older, this is a must.

While I was writing this chapter I had the chance to meet up with Natalie who is the owner of a beauty therapy boutique I used to go to before I moved out of the area. She is lovely and bubbly and has great passion for life and her business. We are very like minded and she also loves what she does everyday having built a very successful business. I had decided to pop in and say hello as I had been meaning to for a long time but my schedule had been so manic. The "pop in" lasted over two hours and was full of fabulous fun business talk. We decided we must see each other on a more regular basis. We both had the same unstoppable drive and passion for our business.

In the next several weeks to follow, Natalie asked me to be one of her resident reviewers, for her new business *"Real Beauty Reviews"*, which was officially launching soon, but already a huge success online. I thought it would be an awesome opportunity as I love all things girly, and I love working with passionate people! What really appealed to me with her business was it helped women from all over the globe. Offering advice, recommendations and most importantly, peace of mind on many different products. I loved that!

One day when I had popped in to pick up some new products I met a young lady called Charde. She is a successful and very talented Kiwi comedian with shows on TV, and an entrepreneur. Such a sweetie, very down to earth and incredibly passionate at only twenty two years old. We had an awesome talk about her career, this book, fashion and lots more. We became instant friends, already having some ideas to work together in the future.

Funnily enough, I was also coming to the end of this chapter when it all came together.

Oh dear, sidetracked ...again. Can't wait for the amazing products from all over the globe that I will have the opportunity to review.

So once again, that was all my beauty favs. Maybe you can give one of them a go if you are wanting to try something different. I often get asked, what I use in the beauty department, so thought it would be a useful wee chapter to pop inside these covers. I always ask people what they use, if something in particular about them catches my eye. Right, off we go now, to the next tips.

Looking cool n classy in the air

When a young mum I didn't have the opportunity to travel. When my kids were older, and after I had walked away from my corporate career, it was then that I started my amazing adventure. My brand is now taking me all over the world, and it is from these travels, when on a plane (when unable to sleep!), I scribbled down my little tips, which you are now reading.

Being a Kiwi girl with a mix of Greek, I do love the more natural Kiwi look, with my touch of Greek as a standout feature, being either the lips or eyes. I soon learnt that when travelling, my comfort won over and not the looking super cute whilst getting on and off a plane. So I tried to think how I could have both. One must always try to look cool and classy no matter what you are doing or where you are going. You know it.

I am all for a set of gorgeous lashes or a stunning super thick and lash curling mascara. Just don't wash them all off in the shower! I discovered this way you can keep the heaviness off your face so your skin has a chance to breathe, then if you want, just before landing you can pop on some foundation or bronzer. Add some gloss/lippy with a touch of color, and so you'll look as fresh as a daisy when you hop off. This is especially important if you are going straight into a meeting after reaching your destination.

Otherwise, I just brush over with bronzer and some lip gloss for a ready to go look to match my stand out eyes. Get yourself a fabulous double sided travel mirror, so you can make sure of the lighting, which is hit and miss on a plane, so that you end up with a smooth, lovely and even look. Nothing worse than a heavy foundation spot or two. Sheesh no.

If you can have your eyes popping with fab lashes, the focus is on them so you don't need to worry about applying liner. You can also wake up ready to go and keep going into the night if need be by just adding the rest.

If you are not a lash girl – my ultimate mascara, the next best thing, and mentioned in my "One and Only's", or the other option is that you just go bare and take sunnies or a hat in case you have tired eyes to cover (like me as I am a complete owl on a plane!).

I now wear flats for all the walking between gates but of course have my heels in my bag/carry on, ready to meet the outside world. As I am always traveling from NZ, which is on the other side of the world to where I usually need to go, there are always connecting flights, and walking through the airports. My first trip away, I only had heels and could barely walk at the end of it. So think of choosing a cool larger shoulder bag to go with your outfit, so you can fit in the extras. A cute and sassy little pair of comfy slippers or some soft fluffy socks, for the long haul, is a comfort must. I will never forget the flight with the guy, who after dinner, put on some Micky mouse pjs and was very proudly and comfortably walking up and down the aisle when he needed to. I am all for comfort but it takes some balls to do that. You go mate, that was really rocking it.

I will always wear a relaxed fit style of clothing so I can be comfy. I go for skinny jeans with stretch, unless they are a boyfriend fit. Add a simple classy lose fit shirt/top, and a cute blazer if needed for the cooler weather.

A bold colored or patterned light scarf and you are complete. Or, I will wear a favorite flared cut frock with wrinkle free fabric, another comfy option and great for the warmer weather. Pull your pumps out of your bag when you land and you are ready for action. I add simple gold bangles and studs for a classy casual accessorized look when I travel, being partial to gold and bling, so these and a diamond or two always comes into the mix.

You may already have your LBB (little black bag) inside your bag with your backup fashion emergency items. So you may have a couple of the below already on hand. The following list comprises of travel extras I would recommend for in the air. It's so great to know you have your options to help you out. Between your carry on and your bag you will have plenty of room, as the majority of these are in travel size anyway.

- Eye mask/beanie
- Ear plugs (yes the airplanes provide these but when you have your own that you know fit and work properly, I think it's worth it)
- Light shawl (if you prefer your own instead of the airplane ones)
- Comfy socks/slippers

Passion, Fashion & Heart

- Silky scarves great for poshing up an outfit also works to pull over hair in the rain (especially with hair that frizzes when wet!)
- Rescue remedy
- Lip balm/moisturizer
- Set of backup temporary lashes if wearing falsies
- Day/night cream/oil
- Shoes (heels for when landed if you are a heel girl)
- Extra layer, e.g. blazer or cardigan, something wrinkle free
- Travel size packet tissues/cotton buds
- Deodorant/perfume
- Makeup purse with all your usual goodies
- Pluckers – for those stray hair you hadn't plucked earlier
- Sunnies/hat for those possible tired eyes
- Something to read, pad and pen, iPad
- Adapter plug for when you hit your hotel (not all have them). And for that country.
- Hair ties to put up in a lazy bun if you feel the need and some clips
- Toothpaste brush/mouth freshener
- Nail touch up kit
- Face spritzer
- Small double sided makeup mirror
- Airplanes seem to have either cranked up aircon, where you're teeth are chattering all by themsleves or boiling hot and you are wanting to rip everything off (not recommended). So I take a beanie hat to keep warm for the cold plane that also can be pulled over the eyes as a blackout to sleep. A super cute delicate knit one of course. I used that on my first NYC plane journey. You may look a little weird but comfort… right. I just don't feel like the masks always do it for me.

- If you are feeling a little sticky, take a freshener towel in your bag to dab your face and neck to refresh. A spritzer is even easier. This is only best if you have a makeup free face – the last thing you want is to have panda eyes and streaky foundation, looking like you have just left the set of, *"The walking dead"* tv program.

So there we have it, just a few tips of mine for when you are up in the sky… hopefully on your way to some exciting new adventure or holiday. You are totally welcome my beautiful friend.

My shopping tips, ideas, and advice

Of course, we all have our totally impulsive shops where one minute we are at home and the next we find ourselves driving to the mall. Don't we? Well for me that was some time ago now as everyday I get to shop in my own shop! 'We have all had those shops' alone and with friends. BUT if you have a "need" list and you are on a budget, I would advise a planned option. When are you going? Where are you going? What do you need? How long do you have?

- Dress in something chic and classy of course, but also a garment that is easy to get in and out of.

- Put your yes no and never ever notebook in your bag ready to go (if it's not already there) for checking your styles for your shape

- List what to buy. I am a list maker so a "what I need to buy list" is a great idea if there are certain things you are looking for and want to stay focused. Also, it is a help if you are on a budget you need to stick to.

- Make sure you are fed and watered before going. There is nothing worse than being on a roll and having to stop because you're starving and starting to fade. Bad and impulsive decisions are made on an empty stomach and when you are a little flat. This could also involve having to dash out to the letterbox to get the credit card bill before hubby gets there first! Remember to put some fuel in your tank so you can keep on going, like the Duracell bunny battery.

- Think about who you will take shopping with you. It also depends on the type of shopping trip it is. You will know who of your friends is best for a specific shop. There is most often THAT friend who you love ever so dearly, and is your total partner in crime but is not quite so practical to work through a list with you.

- If you have the option, shop in the mornings, as it is normally less crowded, the racks are full, nice and tidy, and the sales associates have just had their coffee! Lunchtime shopping is always chaotic as everyone is out and trying to squeeze in a shop before going back to work.

- If a particular item catches your eye, try it on. As now you know what body shape you are, you will only be scanning for certain styles. If you find ten things in your style for your shape. Take them all in, it's part of the fun.

- Don't hesitate to ask for assistance from store people.

- If it doesn't rock your boat, don't get it. Don't settle, you will fall in love with the right thing.

- Don't just get something because it is BOGO (buy one get one free, etc.).

- If you can't decide between the red one and the blue one and they are right for your body shape, get them both if you can. You want options in your new body shape closet, we don't want you starting back to old styles if you don't have enough.

- Don't be afraid to try different sizes until the fit feels and looks right. All brands have different sizing so don't just assume if it isn't in your normal size the game is over. Try another size in the same brand to be sure. It's about the fit, not the size.

- Save receipts. Check store's return policy just in case you get it wrong.

- Shopping solo is a great idea when you want to feel you have the freedom to go into all the stores you want to go in. If you have specific things you need to get, you may find it easier to do it alone. As fun as it is having the girls with you (and you love them to death), you don't always get to go into every store you want to.

- Only buy clothes that are your body shape styles and are comfortable, no matter how cute they are or how much they are marked down. Don't be tempted! Get out your Yes, No and Never Ever notebook we have already talked about to remind yourself what you need to be shopping for. Then there is no chance of guessing and being tempted by old habits.

- If you want to be super organized and maybe get in on a few sale items shopping out of season is a great way to do it. As you probably already know there can be some great new season sales early.

- If a few days have passed, and you can't stop thinking about that one piece you didn't buy, you are having some "should have" moments, go back and get it. It has your name all over it. Life's too short to not get what you love.

- Lastly, but most importantly, HAVE FUN! Now you know your body shape and the styles to look for, it's easy. No more aimless wandering around each store, rifling through the racks, flick, flick, flick, trying lots of things on that didn't fit you right and then walking out as flat as a pancake because you found nothing you liked. Then on top of that, as you tried on all the wrong styles that did not flatter your body, you are now feeling yuk about your body too. NO MORE GIRL. You have got this, remember all we have talked about.

Have that super cute little notebook handy so when you are feeling overwhelmed with what and where you can remind yourself what your body loves.

Before you know it, you will be walking out of that store swinging bags of delicious, heavenly new garments, in your perfect colors, and your perfect styles. All you have to do now is throw open your closet doors and hang those treasures up and plan your next date to wear them.

"Nothing haunts us like the things we didn't buy"

From sunrise to sunset

What to take to work or change up, to turn your outfit from a day look into a super chic and sassy night one. This saves you having to go home to get changed before going out.

So you want something to wear one day that can also carry you through to the evening – here are some great and easy options to make an outfit work for you in this scenario.

Accessories are wonderful in bringing a look together to make it cohesive.

In this case by adding some dangly or big earrings, maybe with a little pop of bling or color will make a change to your outfit. I only ever go dangly earrings OR necklace I don't ever do the both. Just a personal choice as I feel it is a little too much with earrings and necklace especially if statement pieces.

- A necklace, especially for going out, looks dressier. Again go statement, something to posh up the area to give it that after dark feel. I always recommend gold and bling.

- By adding a stack of bangles, or one chunky piece can make a difference to the overall look, and if you are pairing it up with same style or colors in the necklace or earrings, even better.

- Belts are always great for a dress, skirt or pants. A classy little belt in print or color is a great jazzier. For e.g., if you have had a suit look on all day, you could just wear your shirt and pants, pop on a super classy belt, let's say one with a gold buckle, add a chunky gold necklace up top to complete the balance. I love this look. Also works fab for jeans (if your work clothing is more casual). Just add pumps and you are fab to go.

- Adding a little crop jacket or blazer is something I love. Either adding or removing depending on the look, and also the weather, can really work. I love crop jackets in color, they add a super pop to an outfit. They also look chic over a dress or with skirt and pants. If you can tie it in with your heels then you have a fun and classy look.

- Heels can take an outfit from day to night instantly. As you know by now I am totally a heel girl! Love, love and love them. Some people find it amusing as I'm either at the horse paddock in my gumboots or in heels. Slight extreme there, but it's always been that way. I'm a country and a city girl rolled into one. So by adding a different style or color heels, it gives you a brand new look and works for whatever you are wearing. As you will already know, it can take a pair of jeans to a whole new fabulous level. I have always loved either patterned or bold colored heels. And gold of course. As you can imagine I have many, many shoes, then of course I have all the runway shoes too from all the collections.

  I guess I should be thankful that the runway shoes are always too big for me, as I wear quite a small shoe size. Am I thankful? No, not really, as then I could wear all those too! Oh my, what a divine thought. I literally have a shoe shop in my home. I must confess that I have a bedroom dedicated to just all the extras. Umm, and some of mine when the walk in becomes jammed full... shhhhhh... it really is quite wonderful though. I have just noticed that this is the only "add on" that has a paragraph double the size of all the others. But of course… you can never get sick of talking shoes.

- Bags can posh things up too. If you are dining out somewhere fancy, add a little sassy clutch or small handbag with a pop of color to tie in with your look. Gold and silver are always great for that. Did I mention I also have a ton of bags as well and beautiful boxes of jewelry? (Of course one must keep all these things from the runway). Oh dear I am starting to sound a little like a fashion hoarder aren't I?

- Hair style – if you have had your hair up all day, let it down and vice versa. For you, after having it the same all day, it will give you a fresh change and feel for the night.

- Makeup additions are a great way to bring in that night look to your outfit. Touch up, by adding more to your eyes, maybe a little smokier and go a little darker or brighter in your lippy. Maybe a fresh coat of mascara is also needed.

- Scarves are fab and incredibly elegant. A little silky number in color or print can really change up a look, whether it is a dress, skirt/pants and top. I love a little knot to the side or a pussy bow center middle, depending on what you are wearing. I have always admired the stewardess look, with their little scarves perfectly positioned. All you need to do then is match it in with your heels and accessories and it will look amazing.

So… if you know that you are going out straight from work one day, pop in a couple of extra things in your bag/car that morning. In the way as mentioned above you can do a lot, you will then have a whole new after dark look. It doesn't take much and it won't take long. Add your own personal style with the extras and have some fun. You can now easily walk from day light into a starry night.

We have now come to the end of our "This and That" chapter, just some little bobs and tidbits for you gorgeous ladies. Each time I thought of what I wanted to include in this book, I always go back to the things I would get a bit stuck on myself, things I wasn't quite sure on over the years before I started this career. Things I would have liked to have known more about. Most times, these are just simple things. I guess one could almost say silly but I feel still are needed. I wanted to keep it simple, easy and fun.

There is nothing worse than wanting to learn or pickup something new, or trying someone else's way of doing things. Then you start reading, and instantly you switch off, and know even if it is interesting to you, there is the question of are you going to be able to follow it and apply it to you, in your world?

Getting back to sharing with you, a dash of that and a sprinkle of this. You may have heard it before, you may not, you may also just need it said in a different way. So take what you will and do what you desire with it. It is there for the offering. From sunrise to sunset. You are welcome.

Its All About Fabulous YOU!

My last words are my wish for you, and my gratitude for my life. These words are on family, what I have learnt along my journey, on putting yourself first and just following your heart.

You will know by now that it is all about you – the sisterhood. Women coming together, knowing that we are amazing creatures, in that, we wear multiple hats in a day – we either run our own or someone else's business… we look after our homes, feed and care for our loved ones… not to mention, we are responsible for growing human beings… we are councilors, lawyers, supporters, debaters, nurses, teachers and more, just by having the title of mother.

We have the right to feel beautiful, to look amazing and be fabulous. We have the right to choose what we want to do with our lives. If you want to paint beautiful pictures then paint. If you want to pick fruit all day then pick fruit. If you want to act on the big screen, take those classes. If you want to travel the world helping others, then get on that plane. If you want to paint someone's nails then paint them in every color of the rainbow. Do what you love to do and if you are not doing it yet, just decide, that yes, you will do it.

Don't settle… you don't have to think "outside the box", remove the box altogether… be outside the box. *Great things never come from comfort zones* (Ben Francia). *Be fearless in the pursuit of what sets your heart on fire* (author unknown).

Those are just a few quotes that I really love. Just take one step at a time, *'one step is worth a hundred years of thinking about it'* (author unknown). So don't look at the big picture and wonder how an earth it will all come together, because then it becomes too overwhelming and nothing moves forward. It will get thrown in the too hard basket. Baby steps, even just writing a list of the things that you would need to do in order to start the ball rolling. It's a step, you have mentally made that decision, and the rest will come. You can totally do this. You have got it.

The scariest thing I did, turned out to be the most amazing thing I ever did. I have also learnt your gut feelings are so crucial to listen to, every time I go with my gut its magic. When I don't, I always regret it straight away and it never seems to work out. I then tell myself off, reminding myself to just trust it. It has your back.

As I have gotten older I have realized the importance of this, and the great thing is, it's already built into us, it's there, so all you have to do is learn to listen.

I always wanted to travel. I was a young busy mum so it didn't ever happen back then, the kids got older, life went on, it got left behind. It was an "oh well, you have a family now." You settle down, get married and have kids and feel that your own life, your passion, your dreams are somehow over. No it shouldn't be. Don't let it be.

Since I chose to do what I love (again), within six weeks I was on a plane to NYC, then what followed were multiple invitations to travel even further around the world. I have always loved writing and within a year of the launch I had started writing. This is my first book, yes this one that you are holding. I have always loved fashion shoots and styling, now I get to choose, plan and style my own designs, throughout the year for my very own photo shoots. The list goes on. I have my dream job and building my dream life.

You will find once you have made that decision to follow your heart, the rest will come, and keep on coming. For myself, it snowballed, and you too will be amazed at how things just keep developing.

Because of Lilika, I am invited to the most amazing events around the world, fashion weeks I would only have dreamt about, opportunities that just keep rolling in, to the point I now have to stop and prioritize. Women from all over the world are buying and wearing the designs that were once just a picture in my head and a sketch on a piece of paper. Believe me it will all come to you, all the opportunities I had and do have land in my lap. They came to me, the doors just continued to open in front of me. I did not try to make things happen, it all just was.

I am a strong believer in things happening for a reason, and what you focus on you get, also that if you are doing something and it is not working, change your approach, try something different. These I guess have been my main "rules" as such that I have without even having to think about them anymore. When it comes to your passion, the door should be swung wide open. I do think though, that there is no point being on the right path and then just sitting there. So these have helped me to know when to move forward with something, you could say really they are just like traffic lights. When to slow down, to park it up, or to take off.

If something doesn't quite work the way you thought it would, it's not a dead end it's just a detour. Don't be flat about it. Press on forward. The best is yet to come. Picture that detour sign, it will still take you to where you want to go. Just in a different way than you had originally planned or thought was best.

Every time a door has closed for a particular thing, without fail, not long after, something else came along... and you know what?... It was SO much better than my original. SO much more then I had ever hoped for. The biggest mistakes I have made in designing have turned out to be the biggest successes. My forced bed rest after my hit and run accident put me in the position that when the invite came through to showcase in Manhattan, I just happened to have a sketch book full of designs ready to go. Now I see it as quite funny, it has become a wonderful habit, that if a door slams shut in my face and it just isn't coming together, I happily wait to see what will come next. Sometimes the best experiences in life are the ones taken while we are on a detour. Be persistent, don't give up, hang in there and it will happen.

When I think back now on the weeks after I had left the safety and security of my corporate career, I had seriously asked myself those three questions I mentioned earlier in the book. It became that much easier, as it made me realize, even more what I wanted and needed to do.

Since a young adult I had always felt like I was searching for something more, a way to better myself, to keep growing, to learn how to be the best I could be. Feeling like I had so much more to give. I still remember the first time I heard Bob Proctor when my kids were younger and I couldn't get enough! He is such an inspirational man and devoted so much of his life to helping others. I soaked it all up like a sponge. I had always been a very positive person by nature, seeing the best in everyone and often nicknamed a 'Pollyanna'.

When I was older I found Bob Proctor again, well I had always known about him of course but it had been many years, since I had actually listened to him speak. It was my Son, who had come home from work one day and handed me a book called the Secret. He told me I must read it, that I would love it and it was 'my kind of thing'. Of course I started reading it straight away, and Bob Proctor was in it. I was hooked, it all just made so much sense to me. Like a bright light had just been switched on. It was after my hit and run accident a few years later while watching Bob on a webinar, that he mentioned this very inspirational and highly successful woman, also a great friend of his- Peggy McColl. Fast forward some time, I was at the end of writing this book when I had an amazing opportunity, one I grabbed excitedly with both hands...for this awesome woman - Peggy has now become my mentor. Remember, there is always something out there for you, waiting for you to take it. So have an open mind and dream big!

My wedding bouquet with Grandmothers brooch, she wore this brooch nearly everyday.

I have amazing parents, and I know I have told you this already. I have an incredible bond with the both of them. I am blessed enough to get to see them most days. My mother and I get to spend special times together on Lilika, memories that I will cherish forever.

Our bond and shared passion for fashion and design is still going strong, the little girl she used to

Dad and I at the paddock visiting Atlas.

Gypsy dress ups on my very first pony Charlie Brown.

take with her to the fabric shops, now takes her. We get inspired together, we laugh a lot together, times when we are manic meeting deadlines, in it all, we are together. She is experiencing with me what she so sadly didn't get to do with her own mother. My grandmother is never far from my thoughts when I am designing, it always feels like she is there with me. The era in which she lived in, and dressed up in, and the photos I have seen of her back then, seem to just thread themselves through my collections. Sometimes without me even realizing it. I am just drawn in. I then look back at what I have created and surprised how that hint of her is there, yet again.

The brooch she used to wear everyday that my mother passed on to me, and (that I also had clipped to my bouquet on my wedding day) sits in my workroom where I design. So I guess she is there with me, with us both.

I am also a daddy's girl, he is my buddy with a fun and cheeky personality. He always has a joke on hand and will do whatever it takes to make people laugh. Wherever he goes, he will try and bring out a smile, always being such a positive influence in my life.

There are days when I will go out to my horse Atlas, for a break from the studio, to get some fresh air, and Dad will come with me. He has always had a special bond with horses, he had four daughters with four ponies! We all rode from a very young age. Mum and Dad would always be there for pony club on the weekends and for all our shows. Looking back I don't know how they did it all.

We would all be up in the dark at 5 a.m at the paddock, I still remember that excitement in

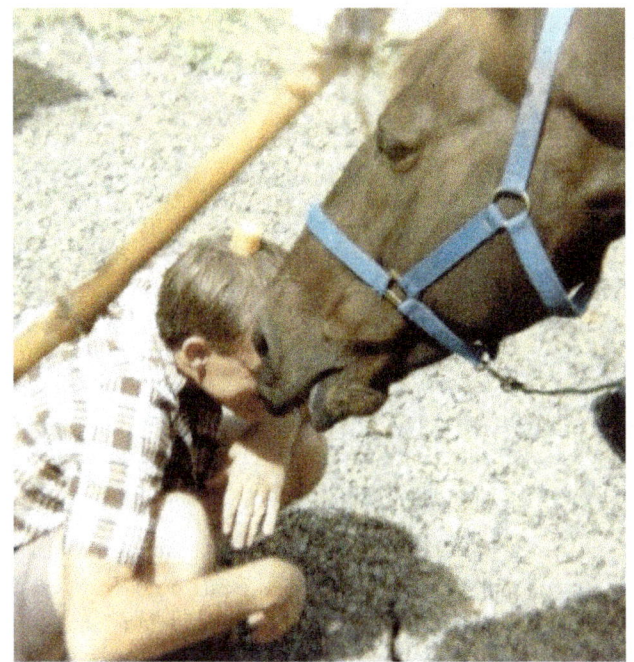

Back in the day, one of my sister's horses eating treats off Dads head.

waking up in pitch black, feeling like we were all on a secret mission. Finding the horses in the dark with our torches. Mum would be plaiting all their tails and manes teetering on her wooden step ladder to reach the top of the mane. She loved the horses but at the same time was a little nervous of them when it got to the back end of the business with the tail plaiting. Her arms were definitely more outstretched then at the top end! She would also make the most beautiful saddle blankets and show covers for all the horses (like she didn't already have enough to do!). We all had our own colors we used for our ponies. Our sets matched perfectly and often had their names embroidered on the corner. For the fancy dress shows, she would also make new sets for the ponies and for us to wear. I still remember my first fancy dress at pony club on my very first pony called Charlie Brown. I was a gypsy and she made me the most beautiful maroon velvet dress. Charlie was dressed up too.

Dad would spoil the horses with treats, when I was young. I remember he would put a piece of carrot or apple on his head and they would gently eat it off the top of his head!

He would talk to them and help groom them. He would float us to where we were going if it was too far away to ride. If we did ride, he would walk beside us and lead if need be. We had wonderful family times together with our ponies and such fond memories to look back on. Going out to the beaches and rivers and taking the horses swimming. Holding on tight to their manes while balancing on their slippery wet backs. There was definitely some scary moments over the years when there was a fall or a bolt!

So horses were a very big part of our lives growing up. I am the only one that carried on riding out of all my sisters. Dad and I love our times at the paddock. Growing up on a farm he has always loved the country, and still talks about his own horse Tom. My daughter also fell in love with horses and she got her first pony when she was ten years old. It was our mother / daughter time, we would have great fun riding together, me on Atlas and she on her pony Cindy. Atlas and Cindy were both in love with each other, which was super cute. If we took Cindy to a show or pony club Atlas would come along for the ride to be with her.

Both my parents have taught me from a young age to just do what I love, to see where my heart took me. I didn't have to take a certain path, even if it may have been something they had wanted me to do. They never put any pressure or swayed me towards one career or another. That gave me confidence by reaching out and trying new things.

I was encouraged and supported in everything I did, they gave me the freedom to be me, to try different things to find out what I truly loved. When it didn't work, they said, 'well at least you gave it a go. You tried and it wasn't for you'. Never the words, 'well that was a failure'.

I have told my kids the same thing growing up, I wanted them to have that same freedom of finding what it is in life, which is their calling, their passion. Today they are both doing what they love. Just because I love designing and fashion it doesn't mean my kids should do it. I am so proud of the amazing, strong, talented, loving adults they have become.

They are, and always will be my inspiration. They are happy in their lives though, because every day they are doing what gives them a fire in their belly, what rocks their boat, and what gives them inner joy. The last thing I would want for them is to be spending it doing something they thought would please me and make me happy. It never works that way in the long run anyway, and we don't have a lot of "long run" in the big picture do we? So let's not waste it.

See, I have always loved writing, like my designing. Lilika opened up the path for me to 'properly' write. Giving me the opportunity through sharing my journey, to express my desire to inspire and empower women through my love for fashion. Now I have started to write I never want to stop! Writing this book has really shown me, my true purpose in life and reminded me of my absolute passion for styling and dressing women. I want to dress YOU. I want to write for YOU. I want to inspire and empower YOU with everything I have. So you can love yourself and live an amazing life that you are in love with!

One thing I have learnt is to be thankful, be thankful for everything and everyday. Not just when you are in a good mood and things are going your way. Find something to be thankful for in the not so great days. Things come to us and happen to us for a reason, to teach us something in some way. I whole heartedly believe this and always have. Every morning I write down five things I am thankful for, and every night I write down five things that I am thankful for, that happened in that day. No matter how small, if you just start with the first one, you will find many more come to mind. If you take a few minutes and do that everyday, you will see the difference in your life.

Now with a Kiwi hug, a Greek kiss. I want to thank you. For letting me sit with you, your cup of tea, hot chocolate or glass of wine in hand, possibly even a chocolate or two as I shared my journey with you. Maybe all the while you are curled up in the most divine, comfortable and silkiest of pajamas.

It really has been fabulous. I truly hope that you have taken something from this book, even if just some laughs at my whirlwind, officially mad, but chaotic and amazing way of life. Maybe you learnt a little something about yourself along the way. Maybe….just maybe, you got out a pen and paper and wrote down what it is you would love to do, if you are not already doing it.

Never forget, it's all about you. Take care of yourself because if you feel great, you will be amazing. You will love more and you will give more to your loved ones, cause you have loved yourself. Treat yourself, pamper yourself. Make sure you have some time for just you. Even if just a hot soapy bubble bath with candles, getting a manicure or buying yourself a beautiful bunch of flowers.

Get to know and love your shape, so then shopping is fun and exciting. You will know what to pull off the rack and run into the changing room with. Then come flying out high fiving the sales girl saying YES! I want one in every color you have!

We are all created with a touch of magic, with unique and beautiful shapes that were made just for us. They have our name on them, nobody else's, they were intended for you and me. Now you know how to highlight them, accentuate them, embrace them, work with them, and most importantly-love them. They are waiting for you to adorn them in the right way, bring out those fabulous parts, bring out not just the princess, but the Queen and let her rule. Put that jewel-encrusted crown on, don't hide her away. Listen to your body, you and she are partners.

So go do it, and make it happen for YOU!

Passion, Fashion & Heart

Your Notes

Christina Kilmister

Your Notes

Passion, Fashion & Heart

Your Notes

Christina Kilmister

Your Notes

For my fabulous readers... my inspiration to write this book... a special offer for you to share the sisterhood Love!

Order *Passion, Fashion and Heart* **today** for someone you think would love to benefit from this special book and you will receive -

4 FREE BONUS GIFTS AUTOMATICALLY!

- 👗 5 simple and easy to use designer tips on what you should wear to elongate your legs.

- 👗 A set of 3 fun and fashionable wallpaper images designed by Christina for your desktop.

- 👗 Discover 7 fantastic must have accessories for your everyday wardrobe.

- 👗 Find out the ultimate swimwear styles for your body shape.

ORDER A COPY OF *Passion, Fashion and Heart* TODAY AND RECEIVE YOUR FABULOUS 4 BONUS GIFTS NOW!

Go to – www.christinakilmister.com

Would you like to receive emails from me monthly with a fashion designer's **insider tip and inspirational quote?** Designed to help you look super special and feel fantastic! If **YES**! - Go to – www.christinakilmister.com and Subscribe Now

If you would like to contact Christina to say hello, discuss any future opportunities, collaborations, up and coming show schedules or current activities please email her at

christina@christinakilmister.com

www.christinakilmister.com

www.ingramcontent.com/pod-product-compliance
Lightning Source LLC
Chambersburg PA
CBHW071910290426
44110CB00013B/1342